Nan'un-do's Contemporary Library

POETRY FOR YOU

(COMPLETE AND UNABRIDGED)

C. DAY LEWIS

EDITED WITH NOTES
BY
Motohiro Fukase
Kaneo Kawada

Tokyo
NAN'UN-DO

C-L10

POETRY FOR YOU　from the original by C. Day Lewis
Basil Blackwell and Mott, Ltd., London
Published in Japan by arrangement with and with full acknowledgment to Messrs. Macmillan and Co. Ltd., London

───────────── 〔別巻録音テープについて〕 ─────────────

本書をもとに, C. Day Lewis 氏の未発表の詩の朗読などをおりこんで構成された録音テープ (頒価 ¥2580) があります。吹込みは著者 C. Day Lewis 氏自身, および, イギリスの新進詩人 Anthony and Ann Thwaite ご夫妻です。音質に多少難がありますが, それは Lewis 氏が高齢, 当時病後であったため, スタジオでの収録が不可能であったためです。なお, このテープ作成にあたり, 奈良女子大学の中沼了先生に多大のご協力をいただきました。ここに記して, 感謝の意を表します。録音個所は次の通りです。

SIDE A: CECIL DAY LEWIS READING.
 1. From Chapter IV ("How a Poem is Made") of *Poetry for You* (pp. 44–50): "The flags, the roundabouts, the gala day."
 2. "O rose, thou art sick!" by William Blake. (P. 81)
 3. "This is the weather the cuckoo likes" by Thomas Hardy. (P. 83)
 4. "Birthday Poem for Thomas Hardy" by C. Day Lewis. 「(P. 94)
 5. "And in the frosty season, when the sun" (from *The Prelude*) by William Wordsworth.
 6. "To the Cuckoo" by William Wordsworth. (P. 84)
 7. "An elegant, shabby, white-washed house" (A Poem on the Irish Home Where I was Born) by C. Day Lewis.
 8. "Here is the unremembered gate . . ." (On visiting my Irish home after fifty years) by C. Day Lewis.
 9. "In a drear-nighted December" (in tow versions) by John Keats.

SIDE B: ANTHONY AND ANN THWAITE READING.
 1. "The Daffodils" by William Wordsworth. (P. 11) (Full)
 2. "Tyger" by William Blake. (P. 30) (Full)
 3. "There was an old Man and he lived in the West" (Anonymous). (P 56.)
 4. "Sir Patrick Spens" (Anonymous). (P. 63) (Full)
 5. "Lord Randal" (Anonymous). (P. 66) 「74)
 6. "Fear no more the heat of the sun" (from *Cymbeline*) by William Shakespeare. (P.
 7. "Have you seen but a bright lily grow" by Ben Jonson. (P. 78) 「(P. 88)
 8. "Unwatch'd the garden bough shall sway" (from *In Memoriam*) by Alfred Tennyson.
 9. "The Hop-Poles" by Edmund Blunden. (P. 95)
10. "Virtue" by George Herbert. (P. 103)
11. "Peace" by Henry Vaughan. (P. 105)
12. "In Time on Plague" by Thomas Nashe. (P. 33) (Full)
13. "At Enoshima" by Anthony Thwaite. (From *The Owl in the Tree*, Oxford, 1963)
14. "Lesson" by Anthony Thwaite. (From *The Stones of Emptiness*, Oxford, 1967)
15. "Love Songs in Age" by Philip Larkin. (Ann Thwaite reading)
16. "Church Going" by Philip Larkin. (Ann Thwaite reading)

まえがき

　この本を高校上級もしくは大学教養課程の英語の教材として翻刻することを思いついたのは、従来わが国の英語の教材が小説に偏して詩や詩の鑑賞に関するものが極めて乏しい事情を考えてその欠を補いたい気持からである。周知のように英文学では昔から詩が文学の王座を占めていて、殊に最近の英文壇には詩の黄金時代といっても決して言い過ぎではないほどの詩的精神の復活現象が認められる。従って詩集や詩論の刊行も応接にいとまのないほどの盛況を呈しているが、われわれの未熟な英語の知識でもってそれらの書物に接してもそう簡単に理解できるものではない。

　この本は現代の英詩人のうち最も有力な詩人の一人でありかつ詩学者でもあり、また最近にオクスフォード大学の「詩学教授」の栄職に就いた C. Day Lewis がイギリスの少年少女のために英詩の味い方を説いた書物であるが、少年少女向きの本であるとはいえ、ここに紹介されている英詩は何も特に少年向きの詩というのではなく、本格的な英詩の世界をなるべく専門的用語を使用しないでいかにして若い世代の軟かい感受性へ伝えるかに苦心を払いながら書かれた書物である。従って英語に未熟な日本の読者にとっては青年が読んでも大人が読んでも立派に通用する本なのである。

　この原本の初版は 1944 年に出て 1951 年までに十二版を重ねている。この本のなかに出てくる英詩の標本はやはり同じ著者の編集した '*The Echoing Green*' と題した三冊の英詩選から選ばれているが、これも 1937 年に初版が出て 1951 年までに七版を重ねている。イギリスの若い世代が現代の代表的詩人の入門書に導かれながら詩を愛する未来の国民として、或いは来るべき大詩人の卵として生長してゆく有様を想像すると、よそごとながら何かしら心の暖まる光景である。

この入門書に興味を感じられた読者は更に進んで，戦前の書物であるが現代の英詩の意味やその将来を非常に面白い筆致で論じた '*A Hope for Poetry*' と題する書物，また戦後ケンブリッジ大学に招かれて講演した '*Poetic Image*' と題する詩論を読まれることをおすすめしたい。Lewis の詩は最近に '*Collected Poems*' と題して一冊本で入手出来るようになった。わが国で出た紹介文については中桐雅夫氏の「危機の詩人」（早川書房，現代芸術選書）をおすすめしたい。前述の '*A Hope for Poetry*' と Lewis の詩の二三についての簡単な説明は「現代の英文学」（弘文堂，アテネ文庫）（深瀬著）のなかで試みたことがある。

なおこの '*Poetry for You*' と '*A Hope for Poetry*' の二書は訳本を準備中なのでもしそれらが無事に実現出来たら参照して載きたい。

　　　1953, 8, 15. 京都にて

註 釈 者

注意: 本文中例えば (II. 58) などの挿入番号は前述の '*The Echoing Green*' の巻数と頁数を示す。

CONTENTS

		Page
	まえがき	i
I	WHAT IS THE USE OF POETRY?	1
II	HOW POETRY BEGAN	15
III	THE INSTRUMENTS OF POETRY	26
IV	HOW A POEM IS MADE	40
V	POEMS THAT TELL A STORY	51
VI	MOODS, VISIONS AND SEASONS	73
VII	POETRY WITH A PURPOSE	99
VIII	POEMS OF YESTERDAY AND TODAY	112
IX	WHEN IS A POEM NOT A POEM?	123
X	HOW TO ENJOY IT	132
	NOTES	141

POETRY FOR YOU

I

WHAT IS THE USE OF POETRY?

A lot of young people—and a lot of grown-ups, too, who ought to know better—ask this question. They are suspicious of poetry. When some one is suspicious of poetry, or painting or music, it is generally because he does not understand them, does not see the point of them. We are always suspicious and a little afraid of things we do not understand. But, instead of admitting this, we are apt to invent reasons for our dislikes which are more complimentary to ourselves. If you ask people who 'have no use for poetry' why they don't like it, they'll probably answer, 'poetry is daft,' 'poetry is soft and unmanly,' or 'poetry won't help you to get on in life, to get a job, to make money.' Let's take these ideas one by one, and see what they amount to.

'Poetry is daft'

People who say poetry is daft are usually frightened of life, frightened of their own feelings and the mysteriousness of the world. Poetry is a special way of using words in order to create a special effect upon the reader and to light up the world for him. If you're afraid of having your feelings stirred in the way poetry can stir them, if you don't want to see more of the world than meets the eye, if you're afraid to see beyond your own nose, then you will certainly avoid poetry as you would avoid a lunatic. But that does not prove that poetry, or poets, are mad. In the old days, people used to think the prophets were mad and throw stones at them: but very often they found out in the long run that the prophets had been right and they themselves wrong. It was the same with the poets. In fact, when you read the Old Testament, you realize that many of the Hebrew prophets *were* poets. From the earliest times, there had been a close connection between poetry and magic; and long after this connection ceased, there still survived a vague notion that the poet had supernatural powers. The ancient Greeks believed that poets were 'possessed' by a god when they wrote poetry: our word 'enthusiasm' comes from a Greek word meaning this very thing— the state of having a god inside you. And people still talk about the poet's 'inspiration,' which means a spirit breathed into him from somewhere outside.

But we must not assume, because of this, that poets are crazy. After all, you don't have to be a poet to feel 'enthusiasm': each of you has moments when he feels a strange, unaccountable excitement welling up inside him, a kind of 'inspiration'; but you don't go whizzing off to the doctor and ask him whether he doesn't think you ought to be put into a lunatic asylum. Some poets do go mad, of course—William Blake, William Cowper, John Clare, Christopher Smart did, and they were all fine poets. The wonder is that more poets don't get queer in the head; for poets carry about inside themselves, so to speak, a specially sensitive apparatus, which can be very easily damaged. But, even when a poet himself seems to be mad, his poetry is often sane—far saner and wiser than the talk of many men who boast that there is 'no nonsense' about them.

'Poetry is soft'

Now that's a most extraordinary thing to say. There's nothing in the world less soft than poetry. A good poem is just about as hard as a diamond: it has to be, or it wouldn't last for centuries and continue to thrill men as keenly as it did when first it was written. Think of the things you know that have the longest lives—yew-trees, tortoises, marble temples, ancient castles. Well, a good poem can live on for centuries longer than a tortoise or a yew-tree; when the castle and the temple are no more than beautiful old ruins, a poem written in the same year as that in which they were built may still be as bright and new as ever.

'All right,' perhaps you're saying, 'I admit poetry

isn't soft. But *poets* are. Every one knows that.' Well, if you think so, you're wrong again. The Elizabethan age was one of the great ages of English poetry: the Elizabethans were a very tough lot of people indeed, but *they* never called their poets soft. Sir Philip Sidney, who told them to give the drink of water to another soldier when he himself was dying, was one of the best Elizabethan poets. In the last war English poets fought gallantly and many of them died. There was one who used to creep into the enemy trenches at night, alone, armed only with a heavy stick, and lay out all the Germans he came across. Another was killed while leading his men across a heavily defended canal in France. Both of these got the Military Cross. In the present war, many of our young poets are fighting, and some have been killed.

But that isn't really the point. The chief reason why it is silly to call poets soft is not because they can fight as bravely as any one else: it is because, to go on writing poetry, you need such great patience and endurance. True poets will go through poverty, despair, the indifference or the flattery of the world, for years and years, in order to produce a good poem. They are never satisfied, always trying to write better. At an age when other men generally retire from work or business, the poet is still working as hard as ever,

WHAT IS THE USE OF POETRY?

to wring the last drop of poetry out of himself before he dies.

'Poetry won't help you to get on in life'

This is the sort of thing superior persons say, or men who think the main object in life is to make money. Poetry, they imply, is all very well for highbrows and people with plenty of time to waste, but it's no use to the man-in-the-street. Now that's a very new-fangled idea. The man-in-the-street in ancient Greece would never have said it: he flocked in crowds to watch poetic drama; and so did the Elizabethan man-in-the-street, to see the poetic plays of Shakespeare and other dramatists of the time. Then think of the mediaeval minstrels and ballad-singers, who drew great audiences in village or castle to hear them recite poems. Think of the peasants in Russia, in Ireland, in Spain, in many other countries, still making up their own poems.

No, it's just untrue to say that poetry has nothing to do with ordinary men and women. And certainly the last thing any Englishman should despise is poetry. Poetry is the greatest glory of our nation, though you don't often find it mentioned in the history books. Your geography book tells you about our exports—iron, coal, woollen goods, etc.—but never mentions that one of our most famous exports is poetry. It *is*, though. Every civilized nation has recognized that poetry is the art in which England excels: our poets are as famous abroad as our sailors and our industrial craftsmen. So the fact that poetry does not help you to 'get on' in life or to make money is no argument for not caring about it, or for being superior about it.

'What's the use of a rainbow?'

We've got rid of some false ideas about poetry; but we still have to try and find out what *is* the use of it. Now, in a way, to ask what is the use of poetry should be as absurd as asking what is the use of a rainbow, or the sea, or a piece of toffee, or a game of football, or a nice dress. A rainbow is a natural phenomenon, the result of the refraction and reflection of the sun's rays in drops of rain. As far as mankind is concerned, it's a perfectly useless object: it certainly won't help any one to make money. Yet the poet who said, 'My heart leaps up when I behold a rainbow in the sky,' only put into words the feeling of wonder and excitement we all have when we see a rainbow. It is something beautiful in its own right, just like a good poem. When you are given a piece of toffee, or a nice dress, you don't sit about wondering what is the use of it: you put the one into your mouth, or your head into the other. You enjoy bathing in the sea on a hot day, or playing a game of football, in just the same way.

WHAT IS THE USE OF POETRY?

Now poetry is, first and foremost, something to be enjoyed—a pleasant experience like bathing or wearing a new dress or eating toffee—and don't let any one tell you anything else. But, just as bathing is more fun if you have learned how to swim and dive, just as a boy will enjoy football more when he knows the finer points of the game, and a girl will get more satisfaction out of a new frock if she has developed a good taste in dress, so you will find a keener pleasure in poetry if you understand what it is aiming at and how it works. The main object of this book is to help you understand the why and the how of poetry.

There are some people who are very fond of poetry but say that, as a form of entertainment, it is obsolete: it was all very well in the days when there were no cinemas, no radio, no cheap books and papers to amuse us, they say, but nowadays competition is so strong that poetry will soon have to go out of business. I shall come back to this argument in a later chapter. First, let us look at the two chief uses of poetry, which no amount of modern inventions can ever affect.

'Bright is the ring of words'

If you are at the sea-side, and you take an old, dull, brown penny and rub it hard for a minute or two with handfuls of wet sand (dry sand is no good), the penny will come out a bright gold colour, looking as clean

and new as the day it was minted. Now poetry has
the same effect on words as wet sand on pennies. In
what seems almost a miraculous way, it brightens up
words that looked dull and ordinary. Thus, poetry
is perpetually 're-creating language.' It does this in
several ways. It may coin new words: it may help
to bring into common use words which, before, had
only been used by experts—technical, scientific words,
for instance: it may put common words into new con-
texts, introduce them to other ordinary words they
had not met before, as a good hostess introduces
strangers to each other at a party and makes them
interest one another: it may enrich the value of words
by giving them new associations—for instance, when
Tennyson, writing a poem about an eagle looking
down from a cliff, said, 'The wrinkled sea beneath him
crawls,' he was able to give a most vivid picture of
what the sea looks like from a great height by bringing
into a new association two quite ordinary words,
'crawled' and 'wrinkled.'

To realize how important a job this perpetual re-
creation of language is, you need only ask yourselves
what words are *for*. They are the chief instruments
by which human beings communicate with one another,
get to know one another, carry on life with one another. We should still be merely animals if we were
all dumb or if mankind had not invented languages.

WHAT IS THE USE OF POETRY?

But words, like any other instruments, must be kept clean and efficient if they are to do their job for civilization. People who treat words in a careless, sloppy way are not properly civilized. Poetry, on the other hand, is an art which has to treat words with care, respect and accuracy.

This does not mean that the language of poetry is something quite different from ordinary speech. Slang is often extremely poetical, because it uses words in a fresh, vigorous way, and makes pictures out of them.

(1) 'I feel tired and limp.'
(2) 'I feel like a bit of chewed string.'
(3) 'I'm terribly depressed.'
(4) 'I feel so low I could crawl under a snake.'
(5) 'The tea is so strong, you could stand a spoon up in it.'
(6) 'It's lovely, strong tea—you could trot a mouse on it.'

Look at these phrases. (2) and (4) are slang ways of saying (1) and (3). They convey the meaning of (1) and (3), but more forcibly because they illustrate it with pictures—of a chewed, limp piece of string and of a man crawling under a snake: (4) does it more effectively than (2) because it is less hackneyed; that is to say, (2) was a vigorous piece of language when first it was used, but it has been used too often and got stale. The same applies to (5); it was once a good, slang way of describing a cup of strong tea, but so many people used it that it has become worn out: (6), which I heard an old Irish countrywoman say, is a far stronger, more vivid expression. (2), (4), (5), and (6) are all slang, but they are also poetic ways of expressing a prose meaning.

I am not saying that poetry is just a glorified form of slang. But it *is* true to say that slang comes from the same source as poetry, from the imagination. And it is interesting to note that, when a nation is young, vigorous, self-confident, its common people generally have a vigorous slang: the Elizabethans had; the cockneys in Queen Victoria's time had; the Americans have today, and so have our men of the R.A.F. Slang is good, then, when it shows that people are using their imaginations, bad when it's a sign of mental laziness.

Two ways of looking at a daffodil

That word 'imagination' brings me to the chief use of poetry, an even more important one than the re-creation of language. When we are very young, the world, nature, people are mysterious to us. Give a baby an orange. He stares at it, fingers it, dribbles on it, drops it, howls for you to pick it up again. To

WHAT IS THE USE OF POETRY? 11

him, it is a beautiful, round, coloured object, with a strange smell, which is heavy to hold and stays put on the floor when he drops it, instead of walking away like the cat. A baby uses all his senses to make such discoveries: he is like an explorer in a new world, full of wonder and surprise at the novelty of everything. In a way, a poet is a man who never grows out of that sense of wonder. It keeps his imagination constantly on the stretch and quivering at the mysteriousness and beauty of the world; and thus his poetry helps *us* to understand the world by sharpening our own senses, by making us more sensitive to life.

Now there are two ways of getting to understand the world—through our heads and through our hearts, our feelings. Science tells us a great deal about how the world works, what it is made of, and so on. Science is the chief way of learning through our heads. But that's not the *only* way of learning about the world —perhaps not even the best way. Let's take a very ordinary object, the common wild daffodil. Here are two ways of describing it:

(1) Narcissus pseudo-narcissus: flower-stalk hollow, two-edged, bearing near its summit a membranous sheath and a single flower: nectary notched and curled at the margin, as long as the sepals and petals.

(2) I wandered lonely as a cloud

That floats on high o'er vales and hills,
When all at once I saw a crowd,
A host of golden daffodils:
Beside the lake, beneath the trees,
Fluttering and dancing in the breeze.

Now, which do you think is the more satisfactory description of daffodils—the scientific one which I have taken from a text book on botany, or the poetic one which comes from a poem by Wordsworth? Many of you would say 'the poetic one,' straight away: and that is, incidentally, a bit of a blow for those who argue that science has made poetry obsolete. Of course, it's not quite fair to compare a scientific description with a poetic one like this, as though they were competing against each other for a prize. Science is concerned with finding out and stating the facts: poetry's task is to give you the look, the smell, the taste, the 'feel' of those facts. Each has its own purpose and reward. But, by contrasting these two descriptions, you can see how poetry and science differ in method. Description (1) is analytic: that is to say, it examines the daffodil as though it was a single object quite separate from every other object which presents itself to our senses, tells us how it is composed, and classifies it. Description (2) relates the daffodils with a number of other things—with trees, a lake, a breeze, and with the poet's feeling of loneliness (at least, he was 'lonely as a cloud' until he met this 'host of golden daffodils').

To make the world your friend

It is the inclusion of *feeling* that makes the difference between poetry and science. Science is not concerned merely with analysing things: it also must try to relate them with each other and thus discover the natural laws at work behind them. But the scientist uses theory, observation and experiment to relate his facts with each other, whereas the poet uses his own feelings, his emotions. It would be all wrong for a scientist to get emotional when he describes a daffodil; and it would be all wrong for a poet *not* to.

There, then, is the great use of poetry. It tells us about the world through our feelings. It sharpens our senses, makes us more keenly and fully aware of life, exercises our imagination and stores up treasure in our memory: once we have seen that 'host of golden daffodils' coloured by the poet's feeling, they will continue for the rest of our lives to 'flash upon that inward eye which is the bliss of solitude.'

Imagine, for a moment, that you are trying to describe one of your friends. It wouldn't be difficult to give the sort of description you hear on the radio when some one has disappeared from his home or the police are after him. You could say he is five foot tall, has blue eyes, a mole on his left cheek, a wooden leg or a red nose. But that would only describe the *outside* of him. It wouldn't tell people what this friend of yours is really like—his habits, his feelings, all the little peculiarities that make him himself and different from every one else. You would find it very difficult indeed to describe the *inside* of him, even though he is such a great friend that you feel you know him through and through. Now good poetry *does* describe life in that way; it tells you about its inside as well as its outside, and thus it helps you to know and love the world as intimately as you know and love a friend.

II

HOW POETRY BEGAN

To find this out, we'll have to jump into a Time Machine, put its gear-lever into reverse, and race backwards through many thousands of years into prehistoric time. Now we've arrived. We're in a clearing in an immense forest. Look at those hairy, ape-like men, stamping in a strange, savage, rhythmical dance round the camp fire. They're your ancestors. As they dance, they mark the beat with cries and grunts and growls, for they've not yet learnt to speak in words, or to sing. What are they doing, those hideous creatures, stamping round the fire in the forest? They're doing magic: they're making a spell. They're doing something else, too, though they don't know it. What you're watching is the very first beginning of poetry: in that rhythmic dancing beat of their feet, in the animal-like sounds they're uttering, and in the magic they're performing, poetry was born.

The earliest men, as you know, were hunters. They had to kill—or be killed—for there were savage animals all round them. At first, they had only their own hands and teeth to kill with: then they invented primitive weapons. At a very early stage, they invented another kind of weapon—a sort of 'secret weapon.' How the idea came into their heads, we do not know for certain: it may have arisen from the use of protective colouring, of camouflage, by the animals which they stalked and which stalked them. At any rate, they got the idea that, if you imitated anything, you gained power over it.

This idea was the beginning of magic, and also the beginning of art—music, poetry, painting, the drama. Before they went out to hunt, these shaggy ancestors of ours would perform a sort of mimic hunt, in which some of them played the parts of the animals and others pretended to be hunting them. The hunters always won, I expect, just as in kids' games the 'English' always beat the 'Germans.' Of course, the real animals weren't affected by this magic: but the men were, for it made them *believe* they were going to kill the animals successfully; and when you believe you're going to win, the battle is half won. No doubt the mimic hunt was good practice, too: in the same way, a kitten plays with a ball of string to train itself for hunting a mouse.

Gods and spirits everywhere

After a while, this mimic hunt became formalized; that is to say, the movements, gestures, sounds were developed into patterns which did not copy the chase

HOW POETRY BEGAN

so closely, but still represented it. But the idea behind it all still persisted. It appeared again when men had learned how to till the earth and get their food from it. For centuries, they held religious ceremonies in the fields—ceremonies which included dancing and rhythmical patterns of words (magic spells again), to make the crops grow and the weather be kind to them. They did this because they believed everything was alive in the same way as they were: they believed there was a god in the thunder, gods in the sun, the rain, the hail, a spirit in every stream and tree and mountain and animal. In some parts of the world, people still believe in fairies—and fairies are the same as nature-spirits.

Poetry, which in the earliest days had this very practical use of helping man (as he believed) to influence and gain power over the forces of nature, still keeps alive the primitive idea that they are somehow *human*: we don't think it at all peculiar when we find in poetry expressions like 'the kindly sun' or 'the cruel, crawling, hungry foam,' though we know that the sun hasn't really a human heart to feel 'kindly' with, nor the foam a stomach to feel 'hungry' with. We find such expressions quite natural, since they convey instinctive feelings which thousands of generations of men have had about nature—that the sun must be kind because it warms us and helps our food to grow, that the sea must be cruel because it drowns people.

How the first poets were made

The earliest poets, like the earliest men, lived almost entirely by instinct. Now one of the strongest instincts of mankind is the instinct to create things, to make things. Originally, no doubt, this instinct arose from man's need to make fires and huts, in order to keep himself and his family warm, to make weapons with which he could protect himself from the wild beasts, and tools with which to till the ground. Our word 'poetry' comes from a Greek word which means both 'doing' and 'making.' And, if we ask how it was that poets first came into existence, the most reasonable answer we can find is that they must have been individuals who were prevented from making and doing practical things like their fellow-tribesmen, and were driven to find some other outlet for the creative instinct, some other way in which they could help their fellows.

Now what could it have been that prevented such people from taking a normal part in the life of the community? There is only one possible answer: they hadn't got the physical strength. Only the strongest men could have much hope of surviving against the harshness of the weather and the dangerous wild beasts. A person who had been maimed while hunting, for instance, or had been born blind or physically weak, was useless to the community—perhaps even a hindrance and a danger to it. But people like this wanted to live, just as much as any one else; and to justify their existence, they invented a new way of being useful. They were not strong enough to hunt, to make things, to till the ground: so they made *images* of things instead—they scratched pictures of wild beasts on the walls of their cave; they made up word-pictures of successful hunts, or 'magic' spells to control sun and rain and bring a good harvest. In doing so, they brought into existence a new faculty—the power of imagination.

'Tell me, where is Fancy bred?'

So the poet's weakness has always been his strength. Homer, one of the greatest poets who ever lived, is said to have been blind. And you know how blind people often are compensated for the loss of sight by developing an extraordinarily acute sense of touch and hearing. In the same way, people who have other physical infirmities—who are lame, for instance, or deaf, or suffer a lot from illness—often become super-sensitive, super-imaginative. This, too, would create the kind of disposition which turns people into poets, story-tellers and artists; for, as I've told you, poets are people who carry about inside themselves a kind of supersensitive apparatus.

Again, if you imagine those earliest poets of all, you will see they must have been rather lonely, must have had a lot of time on their hands, must sometimes have been despised by their fellow men, because they could not take part in the ordinary activities of the tribe. They had more time to observe nature and other human beings. They had more solitude, in which to think and day-dream about them. They were 'out of things': and you all know how, when you are left out of things, when other people ignore you or look down on you, you are apt to make up stories in your head—stories in which you rescue some one from a burning house or stop a runaway train or shoot down a German aeroplane. The making-up of stories in which he was the hero, to compensate for being 'left out of things' in real life, was a most important part of the primitive poet's development. Today we call it 'phantasy,' or 'fancy.'

Of course, the primitive poet was not despised and cold-shouldered all his life. After a while, his fellow tribesmen would recognize that he had a special gift: they would be delighted by the stories he told them in the cave or round the camp fire, impressed by the 'magic' effect of his rhythmical words upon their own feelings. Above all, believing as they did that by imitating something you gained power over it, they

HOW POETRY BEGAN

came to have a great respect for the poet's art, which imitated in sounds and words the forces of nature they had to master if mankind was to survive. So they gave the poet an honoured place in the community.

What sort of stories did these primitive poets make up? It's not difficult to guess. They would describe the prowess of great hunters and warriors; they would tell of exciting events which happened to the tribe: and they would also sing about those nature spirits which they believed to live in every stick and stone, every beast and wood and stream and cloud. They imagined themselves in the role of hero, hunter or nature spirit—'identified' themselves, as we say, with these creatures—and thus developed their own power of imagination. They made up these stories in rhythmical patterns of words, in poetry, because they were better magic and more easily remembered like that.

Hero-worship and legend

Poems of this sort, which tell stories, we now call epic poems, or narrative poems or ballads. I expect most of you have read 'The Ballad of the Revenge' (I. 7), in which Tennyson told the story of a great Elizabethan warrior, Sir Richard Grenville, and his men. Very often the old ballads, however, were not the work of one poet alone. Later poets or even ordinary members of the audience listening to a ballad, would add a stanza here, a few lines there. And pretty often, in their excitement, they exaggerated the deeds of the hero in whose honour the poem was composed. Thus there grew up round these heroes a mass of legend. The early story-poems were, you might say, fiction founded on fact; but the core of them was that kind of hero-worship which you yourselves feel for men and women whose great deeds or fine qualities stir your imagination. When you read about the heroes of ancient times, remember that—but for the poets—they would have been forgotten. Indeed, there was a time when important men used to hire poets to write about them, to make sure they should *not* be forgotten! Poetry, you can see, has a great preservative power: it can make people and things live on for centuries after their ordinary lives are finished, in the same way that creatures are preserved in fossils, or delicate ornaments preserved in the sealed tomb of a Pharaoh, or surgical specimens preserved in alcohol.

Poetry created legends, then. It also created myths. Legends are stories based on the lives of individual men—their struggle against enemies or the forces of nature. Myths are stories which embody some experience or desire common to all humanity. Perhaps the most universal myth of all, which crops up in one form or another in every land, is the Spring-Winter myth.

Myths of the Seasons

If you have lived a whole winter in the country, far from shops and cinemas, kept indoors much of the time, trudging to school through rain and mud and cold, you know what a marvellous relief it is when spring comes. Imagine how much more of a relief it must have been to primitive man. He had no shops or cinemas anyway: he hadn't even got books to read in the long winter evenings; and, if he had had books, there were no lamps to read them by. He was often terribly cold. He worried whether the food he had stored would last him through the winter. Worst of all, he was never *absolutely* sure that summer would return at all. So the first day of spring came as a miracle to him. Now he could be warm again: now he could go out into his fields and need not be afraid of starving.

That passionate desire of his for the end of the winter, that feeling of wonderful relief when the weather at last began to turn warm, echoes through poetry right up to our own day. It is in our blood, so to speak, and that is why so much fine poetry has all through the ages been written about spring. Early man, who always personified (that means 'made people out of') the drama of natural forces, thought of winter and summer, the old year and the new, as enemies engaged in a life-and-death struggle. So he created myths, which describe this struggle in a symbolic way. The most famous of these myths is the story of Persephone, Pluto and Ceres. Persephone, who represents the spirit of growth and vegetation, is kidnapped by Pluto, the god of the underworld. Ceres, her mother, who represents the earth, pleads for Persephone to be allowed to come back to her. A bargain is struck by which Pluto keeps Persephone for six months of the year (winter) and she returns to the earth for the other six (summer).

There are hundreds of variations of this drama. Until quite recently, it was the custom in many English villages to act Mummers' plays at Christmastime. 'Mummers' means 'mimickers,' and the village actors in these plays were mimicking the forces of nature which are engaged in the struggle between winter and summer, the old year and the new, death and life. The pattern behind all these plays is the same. A White Knight, for example, representing summer, is killed by a Black Knight (winter), and then miraculously brought to life by a Doctor or St. George. This bringing-to-life symbolizes, of course, the annual resurrection of the earth (vegetation, crops, etc.) in spring time. The anonymous authors often used to represent winter by a bogy-man figure named after some Public Enemy Number One of their own time. In one play he is Buonaparte; in another, a Turk (which suggests the play may have been written about the time of the Crusades); in others, again, he is called Beelzebub. Often, too, the Mummers blacked their faces. This may be a survival from primitive days, when men were terribly afraid of ghosts and, at certain ceremonies, used to black their faces and disguise themselves in other ways so that the ghosts of the dead should be unable to recognize them and haunt them.

These Mummers' plays are in doggerel verse; and nearly all the nature-myths of the world first grew up in the form of verse. So, from the earliest days, we can see that man used poetry to express his passionate feelings about the world, to comfort himself amid the dangers and hardships of the world, to direct the world's natural forces by prayer and magic to human ends, and to understand the world.

III

THE INSTRUMENTS OF POETRY

Words are the raw material of poetry. The methods that poets use to hammer and shape words into strong, beautiful patterns are called 'poetic technique.' This chapter is going to be about technique—about the craftsmanship of poetry.

You remember, in the Wordsworth poem I quoted, how the poet made us see the daffodils more vividly by linking them up with wind, trees and lake. Poetry is always doing this—making us aware of links or connections between things, which we had not noticed or had not found interesting before. Poetry is always comparing things:

> Shall I compare thee to a summer's day?
> Thou art more lovely and more temperate.
> *(Shakespeare)*

or,
> My love is like a red, red rose
> That's newly sprung in June. *(Burns)*

We're all inclined, when we're excited or angry, to use comparisons in order to express our emotion more vividly. When father is sawing away at a tough bit of

THE INSTRUMENTS OF POETRY

beef, he exclaims, 'This meat's as tough as an old boot.' A boy of twelve, whom I taught once at school, wrote in an essay, 'The autumn leaves were falling like a snowstorm on fire.' That was a comparison any poet would have been proud to have thought of: it's a double-barrelled one; the *colour* of the autumn leaves is reflected in the word 'fire,' and their *movement* and *profusion* as the wind blows them down from the trees are reflected in the word 'snowstorm.' Comparisons like this, where two things are related by the word 'like' or 'as,' are called 'similes.'

Similes can be very simple ('My love is like a red, red rose'): they can be far-fetched ('You've got a face like the back of a bus'—a satisfactory way of insulting somebody, but goodness knows why, for the back of a bus isn't particularly ugly). Or they can be subtle and delicate:

> The winds that will be howling at all hours,
> And are up-gathered now like sleeping flowers.
> (*Wordsworth*)

or,

> ... yet still the sails made on
> A pleasant noise till noon,
> A noise like of a hidden brook
> In the leafy month of June. (*Coleridge*)

Or they can be complicated and at first rather diffi-

cult to take in, like this description by a modern poet
of an air-liner coming in to land at dusk:

> More beautiful and soft than any moth
> With burring furred antennae feeling its huge path
> 5 Through dusk, the air-liner with shut-off engines
> Glides over suburbs . . . (III, 92). (*Spender*)

You see why he compares the aircraft with a moth?
It is coming in at dusk, the time when moths fly most:
its flight, with the engines shut off, is silent as a
10 moth's: it looks rather like a huge moth, in the half-
light: it seems to be feeling its way through the air,
like a moth with its antennae.

Short cuts to big meanings

Whether a simile is simple or complex, its main ob-
15 ject is to compare two things, to set them side by side
in such a way that they light each other up and therefore make us see and understand them more clearly.
Another way of doing this, both in poetry and common speech, is metaphor. When you say some one
20 has 'an iron will' or 'a fiery temper,' you are using a
metaphor. You don't mean that he actually has a bar
of iron called a 'will' somewhere inside his head, or
that you could put your hand into his temper and get
burnt. What you mean is, 'His will is hard and un-
yielding like iron,' and 'his temper is hot as a fire is

THE INSTRUMENTS OF POETRY 29

hot.' In fact, you're using a sort of compressed simile, with the 'like' or the 'as' left out. In a metaphor, the two things compared are not set side by side and linked together by 'like' or 'as': they are fused into a single phrase. A metaphor is a kind of short cut.

The word 'metaphor' means 'transference.' When a seventeenth-century poet, Wotton, called the stars 'You common people of the skies,' he was transferring the ordinary meaning of 'common people' to describe the multitude of the stars, and in the next line we see why he has done it: he goes on 'What are you when the moon shall rise?'—the stars are no more than common people, he is saying, when the moon, the queen of heaven, appears. Another seventeenth-century poet, Vaughan, called death the 'jewel of the just,' which was his way of saying 'If you live a good life, death is nothing to be afraid of; no, it's an adornment, a precious gem; it is the jewelled crown of a good life, for it brings you to heaven.' You see, it has taken me thirty-five words to express—extremely badly—what the poet said in four words. That shows you what a very concentrated thing poetry is: by the use of metaphor, or simile, and by many other devices, it can compress an enormous amount of meaning into a small space. If you doubt this, take any poem you know and try to put its meaning into other words: the beauty and even the sense of the poem will somehow evaporate in the process; which proves, by the way, that you can't separate the *meaning* of a poem from the *pattern of words* in which it is imbedded.

Another device poets use to compress their meaning and enrich their patterns is the epithet. An epithet is an adjective qualifying a noun, your grammar book would tell you, which makes it sound dismally dull: but, when poets use them, epithets are not at all dull— they are surprising and thrilling. Look at Blake's famous lines,

> Tyger! Tyger! burning bright
> In the forests of the night,
> What immortal hand or eye
> Could frame thy fearful symmetry? (II. 101)

The epithet 'fearful' gives you a shock, doesn't it? —as though you'd suddenly come face to face with a real tiger in a dark forest. Or when Keats says,

> Those green-robed senators of mighty woods,
> Tall oaks, branch-charmèd by the earnest stars,

what a magic feeling he gives us by using the words 'branch-charmèd' and 'earnest,' so that we seem to see those branches, dead-still as branches are on a windless night, as if they were in a trance, hypnotized by the steady gaze of the stars. Now look at another tree, the mountain-ash or rowan as Gerard Manley Hopkins describes it:

. . . the beadbonny ash that sits over the burn.
(III. 137)

The epithet 'beadbonny' sounds strange, but exciting. What does it mean? Well, the mountain-ash has bright red berries, which look like beads; and 'bonny' is the Scottish word for 'pretty.' So the poet has coined a new word 'beadbonny,' and into that one nine-letter word he has packed a whole sentence—'pretty with berries that look like red beads.' This new word of his, like most good epithets, is both entrancing and extremely accurate.

Pictures in words

It is a great mistake to think of poetry as something vague and woolly. Poets do sometimes use vague, abstract language; but only in order to make a particular kind of impression on the reader, or to create in the poem a vague, day-dreaming mood. For the most part, poetry uses language in a vivid, precise, concrete way: poetic language has to be quite as accurate as scientific language, otherwise it would not be able to reproduce fine shades of feeling or make us see familiar things, through our imagination, as though we were seeing them for the first time.

To achieve these two purposes, poetry makes frequent use of images. Images are word-pictures, painted by the poet's imagination in such a way as to appeal to the reader's imagination. They are not generally used *simply* to describe or reflect some object which has caught the poet's attention: what they do is to describe that object as coloured by the poet's emotion when he saw it, or by the mood of the poem as a whole. So the images in a poem are not chosen at random; however beautiful an image may be that comes into his head, the poet cannot use it unless it helps to express the emotion of the poem he is writing and unless it can be related with other images in the poem.

Let me show you what I mean by this. In a poem of mine, there are the lines—

>   The bells that chimed above the lake,
>   The swans asleep in the evening's eye—
>   Bright transfers pressed on memory . . .

There you have three separate images (bells, swans, transfers) which go to make a single picture: the thread running through them, and tying them to each other, is the emotion a grown-up person feels when

THE INSTRUMENTS OF POETRY 33

remembering some incident of his own childhood. One of my earliest memories is of sitting up in my pram and watching some swans on a lake, and at the same time hearing the bells of Malvern Priory chiming for evening service. When I was a child, too, I was very fond of playing with transfers—those coloured sheets you moisten and press down on a piece of blank paper, leaving pictures on the paper. You see how those lines got written now? Each of the first two lines contains a separate image, remembered from childhood, and chosen because it helped to build up the mood of the poem: the meaning or 'point' of them is made clear by the line, 'Bright transfers pressed on memory,' which is a metaphorical way of saying, 'Memory is like a blank sheet of white paper upon which life leaves vivid, coloured impressions.'

Now let's take some lines from a poem called 'In Time of Pestilence' by Thomas Nashe.

> Brightness falls from the air,
> Queens have died young and fair,
> Dust hath closed Helen's eye—
> I am sick, I must die.   (II. 1)

Each of the first three lines is an image. First an apparently vague one, which gives us the sad feeling we often get from a sunset (when brightness does in fact fall from the air). The next image is more particular and precise; the poet talks of lovely queens who have died *young*: the third narrows down the theme still further—to Helen, Queen of Troy, the most beautiful woman who ever lived; she too is dead. Running through the three images is the emotion which made the poet write the poem: it comes out in the last line —his fear of dying before his time and his sadness that all lovely things have to perish. I expect you have noticed how very simple the language is in those four lines. Every word is short, simple and ordinary. Yet they are some of the most famous lines in all English poetry.

Te-tumpty-tumpty-tumpty-tum

So far I've been talking about some of the word-shapes out of which poetry is built. But images, metaphors and similes are not the only things which may go to make the pattern of a poem. There are metre and rhyme. You may be surprised that I have not put metre first, after talking so much about poetic rhythm in the last chapter. Well, the fact is that poetry can be made without metre or rhyme, while it cannot be made without that inner excitement which so often comes out in the form of metaphor or image, that poetic spirit which makes lines such as 'Brightness falls from the air' or 'O sunflower, weary of time' glow like jewels: the metre of these two lines doesn't really matter so much; it is their inner radiance, their magic power of evoking a deep emotion in us, that proves their poetic quality.

Some of the finest poetry in the world—that of the Hebrew prophets—is known by us in the form of prose. Isaiah wrote,

> The wilderness and the solitary place shall be glad for them; and the desert shall rejoice, and blossom as the rose. (I. 89)

That has the 'feel' of poetry, hasn't it? But, although its rhythm is beautiful, it is not in metre and has no rhymes. All prose, everything we say, is in some kind of rhythm, remember. And, across even the strictest poetic metres, there is always running the rhythm of ordinary speech. 'To bé or nót to bé— that ís the quéstion': there you have the *metre* of the line. But the *speech-rhythm* of the line, the way you would say it in ordinary conversation, is different; it runs 'To bé or nót to be. Thát is the quéstion.' One of the things that please the ear when we listen to a poem being read aloud is the contrast, the sort of friendly wrestle between its metre and its speech-rhythm: the metre is like a tide pulsing regularly underneath, the speech-rhythm is a less regular movement, like ripples on the surface.

Metre divides a line of poetry into stressed and unstressed syllables; the stresses correspond to the beats in music or the beat of one's feet in dancing—you remember I suggested that poetic rhythm was first created in the dance. Thus, whether the lines in a poem are all of the same length or of different lengths, they will all come within a metrical framework or pattern. Often you find poems divided up into stanzas—that is to say, groups of two, three, four, or more lines with spaces in between them: generally, each stanza in a poem will have the same metrical framework as every other stanza in it, the same number of beats in every corresponding line, and the same pattern of rhymes too.

The more unstressed syllables there are in between the stressed ones, the quicker is the movement of the line. For instance,

> The Assýrian came dówn like a wólf on the fóld.
> (*Byron*)

Here there are two unstressed syllables between each beat, and as a result the poem gallops along at top speed: the poet meant it to go as fast as the Assyrians charging down on their enemy. Contrast that with—

Breák, breák, breák, on thy cóld grây stónes, Ô séa!
(*Tennyson*)

How slowly and sadly that moves! It is a lament, so we expect it to start at a funeral pace. How is this done? There are no unstressed syllables at all in the first half of the line: and, if we say it aloud in speech-rhythm, we should naturally put a strong stress on the word 'grey' and a lighter one on the word 'O,' as well as the metrical stresses already existing on 'cold,' 'stones,' and 'sea': so there would only be two unstressed syllables in the whole line.

The musical pattern

There are many different metres, and variations on metres, which a poet may use. But, whatever metre he is using, the important thing about it is that its stresses create a basic pattern just as the beats in music create a pattern. This pattern is strengthened by the use of rhyme. There are quite a few kinds of rhyme: simple rhymes like 'cat' and 'mat'; two-syllable ones (they are called 'feminine' rhymes), like 'leaving' and 'grieving'; half-rhymes like 'over' and 'fever,' or 'lightly,' and 'frightful,' where only half of a two-syllabled word rhymes. Then you can have assonances—words that, without actually rhyming, have the same sort of sound—'green' and 'grain,' for instance, or 'death' and 'earth.' In an assonance, it is the consonant-sounds only which are alike: in a rhyme, it is the vowel sounds also. One reason why English poets use rhyme so much (the Greek and Latin poets never used it at all) may be that the English language has a special richness of vowel-sounds.

Rhymes, as you know, generally come at the end of lines. They are put there because it helps to create and make clear the musical pattern of the stanza: the ear learns to expect a rhyme, just as it expects a beat, at certain definite intervals, and it's pleased when it finds one there. But you may get a rhyme in the middle of a line, too: and some poets are extremely skilful in making assonances and other sound-echoes all over a poem. This is often done by the use of alliteration. For example,

> I hear lake water lapping with low sounds by the shore;
> (*Yeats*)

Those three 'l's' make a pleasant, liquid sound: the sound here, in fact, corresponds with the sense. So it does in

> Dry clashed his armour in the icy caves,
> (*Tennyson*)

where the hard 'c' of 'clashed' and 'caves' seems to dry one's mouth up when one speaks the line aloud.

THE INSTRUMENTS OF POETRY

Rhyme, assonance, alliteration, the metrical beat—they all have one common factor. It is *repetition*, the repeating of sounds at regular or irregular intervals. Some poems actually repeat whole lines or phrases; when they do this consistently in every stanza, the repetition is called a 'refrain': I expect you have all sung songs in which there is a chorus—a chorus is a kind of refrain, obviously.

Repetition, in this sense, has a special pleasure attached to it—the pleasure of recognition: we get the same pleasant sensation from hearing a sound repeated as we do from recognizing a familiar face amid a crowd of strangers. Now this repeating of sounds, or sometimes of phrases and whole lines, together with the steady beat of the metre, is what makes the musical pattern of a poem. It is connected with the tom-tom beat with which savages accompany their religious rites and dances in the jungle; and it dates back to the making of magic spells. The purpose of this rhythmic repetition is both to excite you and to lull you. That may sound contradictory. But it's true. Poetry must put part of you to sleep in order to wake up and excite another part of you. It puts to sleep the part of you that reasons and argues; it awakens the part that remembers, feels and imagines. For both the putting-to-sleep and the waking-up process, rhythmic repetition of sound is a powerful instrument.

IV
HOW A POEM IS MADE

When I talk to schoolboys and schoolgirls about poetry, they often ask 'What is inspiration?' or 'Do poets have to be inspired before they can write a poem?' or, point-blank, 'Are *you* inspired?' Those are difficult questions to answer (especially the third one!). But I'm going to try and answer them now—to give you some idea of what goes on in a poet's mind when he is composing a poem.

First, you must realize that a great deal of the creating of a poem has already taken place before the poet reaches for his pen and starts writing anything down: and I don't mean by this that he makes up most of the poem 'in his head,' though some poets do. A poem is created by three stages.

1. The seed or germ of a poem strikes the poet's imagination. It may come in the form of a strong but vague feeling, a particular experience, or an idea: sometimes it first appears as an image: perhaps even —as a poetic phrase or a whole line of verse—already clothed in words. The poet jots down the idea or image in his notebook, or just makes a mental note of it. Then he probably forgets all about it.

2. But the seed of the poem has passed into him,

HOW A POEM IS MADE

into the part of him we call 'the unconscious mind.' There it grows and begins to take shape (together, maybe, with other poetic 'seeds,' for a poet may have any number of poems growing inside him at once), till the moment comes when it is ready to be born. For a poem, this second stage may take a few days only or it may take years.

3. The poet feels an urgent desire to write a poem. It's often an actual physical feeling: I myself get it in my stomach; it's like a mixture of the feeling I have there when I'm hungry and the one I have when I'm particularly excited or frightened about something that's just going to happen to me. Now the poem is beginning to be born. The poet sits very quietly—or he may stride all over the countryside at five miles an hour, or go for a ride in a bus—whatever helps him best to concentrate on getting the poem out of himself. He recognizes, in it, the seed which first came to him weeks or months before, which he may have forgotten all about in the meanwhile; but the seed has grown and developed in a remarkable way.

Stage 3 is where the poem bangs at the door, so to speak, and demands to be let out. What comes out first is not the finished poem, though: it is the general shape and idea of the poem, sometimes a whole stanza ready-made, seldom more than that. This is where the hard work of writing a poem begins—and it is very hard work indeed, I can tell you. The poet has to get the rest of the poem out, to shape it, to choose every word in it as carefully as you would choose a cricket bat or a new dress for yourself. Some poems are born more easily than others: but there's nearly always a certain amount of hard work about it, and often it's so hard that the poet may take hours—or even days—to write one single line that really satisfies him.

The coal that glows and fades

So don't get the idea that 'inspiration' means a great golden flood of words pouring into the poet's mind and marshalling themselves neatly into lines and stanzas. Inspiration is when the first seed of a poem strikes root in him. You'll notice I used the phrase 'strikes root': a poet may have many experiences, receive many ideas and images, which *could* be the seeds of poems, but somehow they don't strike root—don't get deep enough into his imagination to fertilize it. And he can never tell *which* of his experiences is going to form itself into a poem, until the poem actually starts asking to be born. We might fairly apply the word 'inspiration' to this moment of the poetic process too—the moment when, with eager excitement, the poet realizes he is ready to create a poem. The best way I can describe this moment is to say that it's rather

HOW A POEM IS MADE

like switching on your radio to get some distant station: you move the dials, oh so delicately, there is a long silence, the instrument begins to warm up, and at last a faint voice is heard—words growing gradually more easy to hear and understand.

Where this inspiration comes from, nobody really knows. But obviously, just as you need a radio set to receive the sound waves sent out by a broadcasting station, so the poet needs a sensitive apparatus inside himself to receive the messages of inspiration. This apparatus is the poetic imagination. Every one possesses some imagination: but the poet's has to be developed in special ways. I described some of these in chapter 2, when I told you how people first became poets. But that's only the beginning of it. You develop a muscle by exercising it. And the poet develops his imagination by exercising it.

He does this partly by writing poetry: he gets into the *habit* of writing poetry, and this habit is one of the things that distinguishes a real professional poet from the person who just writes a poem now and then for fun. He does it, also, by constantly playing with words, just as a conjuror absent-mindedly plays with coins to keep his hand in: you can never be a poet unless you are fascinated by words—their sounds and shapes and meanings—and have them whirling about in your head all the time. Above all, the poet develops his poetic faculty through contemplation—that is to say, by looking steadily both at the world outside him and the things that happen inside him, by using all his senses to *feel* the wonder, the sadness and the excitement of life, and by trying all the time to grasp the mysterious pattern which underlies it. Yet, however devoted he is to his proffession, however much he contemplates and practises, however skilful a craftsman in words he may become, a poet can never command inspiration. It may stay with him for months, or desert him for years. He does not know when it will come—or go. As Shelley said,

> The mind in creation is as a fading coal, which some invisible influence, like an inconstant wind, awakens to transitory brightness.

'The flags, the roundabouts, the gala day'

Now I'm going to take you behind the scenes and show you how one of my own poems was written. I think it will help you to understand what I've just been saying. Here is the poem:

> Children look down upon the morning-gray
> Tissue of mist that veils a valley's lap:
> Their fingers itch to tear it and unwrap
> The flags, the roundabouts, the gala day.
> They watch the spring rise inexhaustibly—

A breathing thread out of the eddied sand,
Sufficient to their day: but half their mind
Is on the sailed and glittering estuary.
Fondly we wish their mist might never break,
Knowing it hides so much that best were hidden: 5
We'd chain them by the spring, lest it should broaden
For them into a quicksand and a wreck.
But they slip through our fingers like the source,
Like mist, like time that has flagged out their course.

The seed of this poem was a strong feeling I had about my own two children. It is a feeling most parents have, at one time or another—a feeling of sadness that their children must grow up, must leave their protection and go out into the dangerous and difficult world. When you are young, you sometimes resent your parents having that feeling: you *want* to grow up and be independent.

Now, if you look at the poem again, you'll see there are two themes, or subjects, in it—the original one, my *own* feeling, which comes out in the last six lines; and the *children's* feeling of impatience and expectation, which comes out in the first eight. These two themes are intended to balance and contrast with each other.

Before I actually start writing a poem, I often find a line of verse comes into my head—a line which gives me a clue to the theme and pattern which the poem will develop: a sort of key-line. When I sat down to begin this sonnet, such a line of verse at once came into my head. That line (it is the only one I didn't have to work for) was 'The flags, the roundabouts, the gala day.' I thought about this line, and saw that it was an image of a fête or a fair, the sort of thing a child looks forward to; obviously, it symbolized (that is, 'stood for') the grown-up world which a child is so impatient to enter. The idea of *impatience* then added some more lines—the first three. Here, the early-morning mist covering the valley represents the veil which the children wish to tear away, as they would tear the tissue-paper off a birthday present—the veil which shuts them off from the grown-up world. The image came out of my memory, recalled from a day several years ago when I was taking my children to school in Devonshire, and we paused at the top of a hill and saw the whole of the valley below covered with mist: I remembered thinking at the time that it looked like tissue-paper, but I'd forgotten all about the incident until I began to write this poem.

Next, I wanted a second image-sequence, as a variation on the theme expressed in the first four lines. You'll find it in lines 5 to 8—the picture of a spring bubbling up out of the earth, and children bending down to watch its 'breathing thread.' The word 'breathing' gives you a clue to the meaning of this passage: the spring represents life near its source, *young* life; and the children are only half satisfied with it; 'half their mind' is looking forward to the time when their life will have broadened out, as a stream broadens into an estuary, and become more important and exciting. The image of the spring, like that of the mist, came out of my memory: it was a particular spring, near a country house in Ireland, which used to fascinate me as a child; I remember spending hours watching it, wondering how such a tiny thread of water managed to force its way out of the earth.

Next, the other theme had to be started—the *parents'* feeling about the children going out into the world. Notice that, although this theme was the original seed of the poem, it now occupies a relatively small space (lines 9 to 12): it often happens, when you are writing a poem, that you find the poem turning out quite differently from what you expected—in other words, you don't know what a poem is going to be like till you have gone some way with the composing of it; indeed, to a certain extent, a poem *composes itself*. Lines 9–12 say, quite simply, 'We grown-ups wish the mist of childhood might never break for our children, because, when it does, they'll see the world is not such a pleasant place as they imagined. We'd like to chain them to their childhood, to save them from being hurt ("a quicksand and a wreck") as every one must sometimes be hurt by life when he grows up.' But the poem couldn't end like that, could it? After all, a parent can't really prevent his children growing up, even if it was right for him to try and do so—which it isn't. So, in the last two lines, I describe how children grow independent of their parents, slipping away from them as mist or water ('the source') slips through one's fingers: they must fend for themselves, run their own race—and time has already 'flagged out their course.'

A corridor of mirrors

I wonder whether you have noticed something about those last six lines. Except for the quicksand and the wreck there are no new images in them. Even the phrase 'flagged out their course' (which, by the way, is another memory-image of mine, derived from a two-mile steeplechase I ran in as a boy of fourteen)—even this phrase echoes 'the flags' of line 4. Instead of using new images, I have repeated those of the first eight lines—mist, the spring, the estuary ('lest it should *broaden* For them into a quicksand and a wreck'), the flags. In the last chapter I told you how important a part is played in poetry by repetition. It is not only words and phrases, but also images, which can be repeated. And they are repeated in this poem, so that you can see the two main themes from a number of different angles, just as you can see many different reflections of yourself if you walk down a corridor of mirrors.

Lastly, what I have told you about the sources of these particular images will help you to understand how a poem grows. The seed of this poem took root in my mind. Then, without my being aware of it, it somehow attracted to itself several experiences I had had at quite different periods of my life and forgotten about. It got hold of a Devonshire mist, an Irish spring, and a steeplechase course in Dorset; it added an estuary with yachts sailing on it (I still don't know where that last picture came from): and, when I began to write the poem, these four images rose out of my mind all ready to illustrate the theme. . . .

The actual process of writing poetry, then, is rather like the process by which a diamond brooch is made. The poet digs into himself, as a miner digs into a hillside, to find the precious stones—the themes and images of his poems. However skilful and hard-working a miner is, he will not find any diamonds unless there are some to be found there: and you won't get any poetry out of yourself either unless it's there already —unless your imagination is so hot and strong that it has fused your experience into the precious stones which are the raw material of poetry, in the same way as certain chemical conditions are necessary for the making of diamonds beneath the earth's surface. You can't, in fact, write a real poem just by wishing to write one. When the diamonds have been mined, they must be selected, graded and cut before they can be used for an ornament. This process is equivalent to the work a poet has to do to make a finished poem out of the raw material his imagination yields him. And, just as the quality and size of the diamonds available to him affect the *design* of the brooch which the jeweller makes, so the nature and quality of our poetic material help to create the *pattern* of our poem.

V

POEMS THAT TELL A STORY

The first poem many of us hear in our lives is a nursery-rhyme or a lullaby sung by our mother. When we are small, we love words for their own sake even though we don't understand their meaning. We also love stories. If you think back to the time when you were a child, you will realize how these nursery rhymes appealed to you.

> Hush-a-bye, baby, on the tree top,
> When the wind blows, the cradle will rock,
> When the bough breaks, the cradle will fall,
> Down will come baby, cradle and all.

We loved that, for its rocking rhythm and lullaby words, and because it contains a dramatic little story-picture. We'd still have loved it even if we'd been old enough to think that it was nonsense; for surely it must be—after all, parents don't put their children to sleep in cradles at the tops of trees. Well, *human* parents don't. But what about birds? Is 'Hush-a-bye, baby' a poem about birds in their nests? That's a new idea. You see now, even in the simplest poem there's generally more than meets the eye. A poem may be nonsense; that is to say, its thought and language do not make the same *kind* of sense as we find in ordinary conversation or in prose-writing. But it is very seldom pure nonsense: there is nearly always a meaning beneath the surface of it.

'Hush-a-bye, baby' has a story in it. So has that comic cockney nursery rhyme which goes—

> Eaper Weaper, chimbley-sweeper,
> Had a wife but couldn't keep her,
> Had anovver, didn't love her,
> Up the chimbley he did shove her. (I. 19)

More nonsense? Or is it, maybe, a poetic story founded on fact, on a true story of some villainous chimney-sweep who murdered his wife and shoved her body up the chimney? Some of the most beautiful nursery rhymes hardly seem to make any sort of sense at all: 'A pin to look at a peep-show' (I. 3) and 'How many miles to Babylon' (I. 37) are like this. But, if we could go back into history and talk to the people who made them up, we should find there was a story at the bottom of them. Some nursery-rhymes we know to have been really political poems: they were composed by people who, for fear of persecution, didn't dare to attack their rulers openly in words; so they made up rhymes which *seemed* to be harmless nonsense,

POEMS THAT TELL A STORY

but would be understood by their friends. 'Georgie-Porgie, pudding and pie' is one of these. They were a kind of code-writing, and people in the Occupied Countries during the war have been doing the very same thing.

Gossip into poetry

Our nursery-rhymes and nonsense rhymes, then, have some resemblance to the magic spells which primitive men made up. Savages, like children, enjoy words for their sound, and have a great feeling for the mysteriousness of the world. Magic spells used rhythmical jumbles of words to express this sense of mystery and to influence the powers of nature. As men became a little more civilized, a kind of poetry grew up which is half-way between the nonsense verse and the more logical story-poems that we call 'ballads'. This half-way poetry is folksong. As the name suggests, it is poetry made up by the folk (the common people) for folk to sing.

If you read some folk-songs, you will notice three things about them: they are strongly rhythmical; they tell a story; they very often have a chorus, or refrain. For instance, there is 'A farmer he lived in the West Country' (I. 1). This poem has a swinging, bouncing sort of rhythm, and it tells the story of a jealous girl who pushed her youngest sister into a river. Here are the first two stanzas of it. Notice how the straightforward story of the poem is mixed up with what seems to be nonsense—the refrains in the second, fifth and sixth lines of each stanza. Sense and nonsense are put together here, blending to a rhythmical pattern.

> A farmer he lived in the West country,
>   Bow down! Bow down!
> A farmer he lived in the West country
> And he had daughters one, two and three,
> Singing 'I will be true unto my love
> If my love will be true unto me.'
>
> One day they walked by the river's brim,
>   Bow down! Bow down!
> One day they walked by the river's brim
> When the eldest pushed the youngest in,
> Singing 'I will be true unto my love
> If my love will be true unto me.'

Another famous folk-song, 'The Wraggle Taggle Gipsies' (I. 80), describes how a fine lady ran away from her husband to join a gipsy band. Then—the reverse of this—there is a folk-song about the son of a humble broom-cutter who married the lady of the castle (II. 92). Or the grand old one about Admiral Benbow—

POEMS THAT TELL A STORY

Brave Benbow lost his legs by chain-shot, by chain-shot,
Brave Benbow lost his legs by chain-shot:
Brave Benbow lost his legs, and all on his stumps he begs—
Fight on my English lads, 'tis our lot, 'tis our lot. (II. 20)

The first three poems I mentioned are rather like fairy tales in verse. But folk-songs differ from fairy tales in being more firmly based on fact. Admiral Benbow we know really existed. But so, I believe, did the lady who ran away with the gipsies, and the broom-cutter's son, and the nasty girl who pushed her sister into the river. The 'folk,' whether they work in field or in factory (but particularly if they are country folk), live pretty uneventful lives on the whole. Therefore, they are greatly excited by any unusual event that happens in the neighbourhood, and gossip about it for years after it has taken place. Folk-songs are often just gossip turned into poetry. Our folk-song flourished most when the great majority of people were living on the land, in villages which were cut off from each other and from the towns—no buses, no newspapers, no radio: and the story of the broom-cutter's son who married the lady of the castle, for instance, which nowadays might get half a column in the local newspaper, in those olden times was given a far longer life by being put into verse and sung by the villagers.

As if it had happened to us

This, by the way, illustrates an important point about poetry, as compared with prose. You and I wouldn't be much excited by an old newspaper cutting which read:

LOCAL BOY MAKES GOOD

Last Thursday, at Haughty Castle, were celebrated the nuptials of Lady Superba Fitzhaughty and Mr. Jack Smith. This event was the culmination of a whirlwind romance between a distinguished and beautiful representative of one of our oldest county families, and a highly respected young broom-cutter. Speaking at the wedding reception, the bridegroom's father Mr. A. Smith, who is also in the broom-cutting business, said, 'If any further proof were needed that we live in a democratic age, it would be supplied by the event which we are celebrating to-day,' etc., etc.

At least, we shouldn't be much interested in it unless we knew the people concerned. But we *are* excited when we read:

There was an old man and he lived in the West,
And his trade was the cutting of broom, green broom;
And he had a lazy lad, whose name it was Jack,
Who'd lie in his bed till noon, till noon,
Who'd lie in his bed till noon.

The old man arose and to his son goes,

And swore he would fire the room, the room,
If Jack wouldna rise and sharp up his knives
And go to the wood to cut broom, green broom,
And go to the wood to cut broom.

Then Jack he arose and put on his clothes;
He banned and he swore and did fume, did fume,
To think that he should, with his breeding so good,
Be doomed all his life to cut broom, green broom,
Be doomed all his life to cut broom.

So Jack he passed on to the Greenwood alone,
Till he came to a castle of gloom, grey gloom;
He rapped at the gate where'er he could beat,
Crying 'Maids, will you buy my green broom, green broom?'
Crying 'Maids, will you buy my green broom?'

A lady on high did him then espy,
And marvelling much at his bloom, bright bloom,
She called on her maid to use all her speed
And bring up the youth with his broom, green broom,
And bring up the youth with his broom.

Jack climbed the dark stair without dread or fear,
Till he came to this fair lady's room, fine room;
With courtesy kind he pleased so her mind,
She asked him there for her groom, bridegroom,
She asked him there for her groom.

Now all ye broom-cutters that live in the West,
Pray call at the castle of gloom, grey gloom;
There's both meat and drink, lads, and what do you
    think?—
No trade like the cutting o' broom, green broom.
No trade like the cutting o' broom.

Anon.

We are excited by this because poetry has the power of making a thing, which happened years ago to people we don't know, seem to be happening to *us*. Poetry, we say, *universalizes* experience: which means that it opens up to every one an experience that was originally the private property, so to speak, of a few people.

Most folk-songs are based on local scandal—violent deeds or unusual events which the composer of them wished to commemorate. But not all of them. Some, for example, were made for special occasions, like 'Wassail and wassail all over the town' (I. 94), which was sung at Christmastime like a carol. Others again, like 'Twelve Oxen' (I. 39), are songs pure and simple.

A few folk-songs are pure nonsense verse, filled with the kind of riddles which country people used to like so much. 'In Nottamun town' (I. 42) is an example of this. Compare it with the opening lines of the Icomb Mummers' Play, and you'll see what I mean.

POEMS THAT TELL A STORY

In comes I Old Hind-before,
I comes fust to open your door.
I comes fust to kick up a dust,
I comes fust to sweep up your house.
I went down a dark, narrow lane,
Weren't very dirty, neither very clean;
I come to Wrought-Iron House
Thatched with brass candlesticks.
There was an Iron Pear Tree before the door,
I knocked at the Door and the Maid came out.
I asked her one, and she gave me one
As hard as a blacksmith's anvil.
I returned her many thanks.
She asked me to have a crust of her ale
And a glass of her bread and cheese.
I said, 'Yes thanks,' but I meant 'No please.'
I went down a little bit further,
I come to two men threshing Bacca-Carns,
One hit a rearing blow, t'other hit a driving blow,
Which cut a Bacca-Carn through a nine-inch wall,
Killed a dead dog t'other side,
The dog jumps up and hollows Bow-wow-wow.
I took me dog without his tail,
And loaded me gun with a long spiked nail.
I met a man, he fled with glee;
I nailed his shadow to a tree.
I've travelled here, I've travelled there;
I should like to taste a drop of your strong beer.

(III. 47) (*From the Icomb Mummers' Play*)

Those lines are full of the countryman's primitive, riddling humour. They are spoken by the actor who introduces the play, and they end up with a request for a glass of beer. Although the lines are as crazy as anything in ITMA, they have a poetic quality about them: and two lines in particular—'I met a man, he fled with glee; I nailed his shadow to a tree'—give me the same kind of thrill that I get from a ghost story.

To return to the more common type of folk-song: here is one from the United States, called 'Casey Jones,' which records a terrible accident that occurred in the early days of American railways. It was a head-on collision between two trains, caused by the failure of a pointsman to switch one of them into a siding and allow the other—the Western Mail—to pass by on the single main line.

> Come all you rounders if you want to hear
> The story of a brave engineer;
> Casey Jones was the hogger's name,
> On a big eight-wheeler, boys, he won his fame.
> Caller called Casey at half-past four,
> He kissed his wife at the station door,
> Mounted to the cabin with orders in his hand,
> And took his farewell trip to the promised land.
>
> Casey Jones, he mounted to the cabin,
> Casey Jones, with his orders in his hand!

Casey Jones, he mounted to the cabin,
Took his farewell trip into the promised land.

Put in your water and shovel in your coal,
Put your head out the window, watch the drivers roll,
I'll run her till she leaves the rail,
'Cause we're eight hours late with the Western Mail!
He looked at his watch and his watch was slow,
Looked at the water and the water was low,
Turned to his fireboy and said,
'We'll get to 'Frisco, but we'll all be dead!'
                (*Refrain*)

Casey pulled up Reno Hill,
Tooted for the crossing with an awful shrill,
Snakes all knew by the engine's moans
That the hogger at the throttle was Casey Jones.
He pulled up short two miles from the place,
Number Four stared him right in face,
Turned to his fireboy, said, 'You'd better jump,
'Cause there's two locomotives that's going to bump!'
                (*Refrain*)

Casey said, just before he died,
'There's two more roads I'd like to ride.'
Fireboy said, 'What can they be?'
'The Rio Grande and the Old S.P.'
Mrs. Jones sat on her bed a-sighing,
Got a pink that Casey was dying,
Said 'Go to bed, children; hush your crying,
'Cause you'll get another papa on the Salt Lake line.'

Casey Jones! Got another papa!
Casey Jones, on the Salt Lake Line!
Casey Jones! Got another papa!
Got another papa on the Salt Lake Line!

There are several things worth noticing in that poem. First, the free, vigorous metre, with its underlying rhythm panting away like the exhaust of a powerful engine (you can *hear* the engine labouring up a steep gradient in 'Cásey púlled up Réno Híll'). Second, the catchy refrain, typical of good folk-song in spite of its unusual subject. Third, the dramatic way in which the story is told: there is no description of the accident itself; you may be a bit disappointed by this at first, but you soon realize that the poem is much more exciting because it breaks off at the critical moment when two locomotives are 'going to bump.' 'Casey Jones' is a folk-song, with a tune of its own; but it also has the dramatic technique of a ballad—a technique which, as you will now see, depends almost as much upon what is *left out* as upon what is put in.

'A plume in his helmet, a sword at his knee'

Ballads are like most folk-songs in that they tell a story. But, whereas the latter were always sung (we still know the old tunes for nearly all our folk-songs), ballads were generally recited. There is a special ballad metre, in which the great majority of ballads are written, designed for simplicity and speed:

> Now Robin Hood is to Nottingham gone,
> With a link a down and a day,
> And there he met a silly old woman,
> Was weeping on the way. (I. 65)

The metre is simple, because—as I told you before—the ballads were composed by simple people, and often members of the audience liked to make up additional stanzas. It is a fast-moving metre because a ballad generally had quite a long story to tell, and it was necessary to keep it on the go so that the listeners shouldn't get bored. It is also a flexible metre: that is to say, it allows considerable variation of rhythm, as the stanza I have just quoted shows.

The ballads are flexible, not only in their metre, but in the way they tell their stories. They tell them in a highly dramatic way; and the dramatic technique they use has something in common with the movies. For example, here are two consecutive stanzas from the famous ballad of 'Sir Patrick Spens' (II. 58):

> I saw the new moon late yestreen,
> Wi' the auld moon in her arm;
> And if we gang to sea, master,
> I fear we'll come to harm!

> They hadna sailed a league, a league,
> A league but barely three,
> When the lift grew dark, and the wind blew loud,
> And gurly grew the sea.

In the first stanza, one of the crew is telling the ship's owner that bad weather is coming and it would be dangerous to put to sea. Then, instead of going on with the argument that must have taken place between the owner and the crew and describing how in the end the ship actually sails, the poem takes a jump: in the next stanza, the ship is already at sea, nearly three leagues from land, and the storm is blowing up. We noticed the same kind of jump in 'Casey Jones,'—after 'two locomotives that's going to bump.'

The same dramatic device is constantly used in the movies—we've got so used to it that we don't even notice it nowadays. The hero, say, gets on to a train at Chicago: there is, perhaps, a shot of the wheels going round and the coupling-rod gathering speed: and the next thing we see is the hero getting out at New York. There obviously isn't time in a film, any more than in a ballad, to show everything that happens to the characters: therefore only the most dramatic, exciting things are described, and it is left to our imagination to fill in the gaps. Another way in which the ballad-writers speeded up their stories was by leaving out 'he said' and 'he replied' when two people are talking. But, of course, they do not keep their story going at top speed all the time: here and there they slow it down, as you will see in the verbal repetition (common in ballads) at the beginning of stanza 2 above; this slowing-down increases the dramatic tension of the poem.

'Of moving accidents by flood and field'

The ballad of 'Sir Patrick Spens' is about a shipwreck which is mentioned in the history-books. Quite a number of ballads are founded on historical events: one of the greatest of these is 'Chevy Chase' (II. 75); and there is a whole collection of ballads—you will find them in the *Oxford Book of Ballads*—about Robin Hood. The Robin Hood ballads are the best ones to begin with, as they are in more or less ordinary English. The great majority of our finest ballads, however, were composed by people living near the Border, and are therefore a mixture of English and Scots dialect, which makes them a bit difficult to follow. The best thing is to get a grown-up to read a few aloud to you first; then you will get into the swing of it and be able to read them by yourself. You'll certainly miss a great deal by not reading them, for they tell the strangest, most exciting stories.

The great mass of ballads deal with adventures and

violent deeds—what Othello called 'moving accidents by flood and field.' One of my own favourites is 'Lord Randal,' which is about a young man poisoned, together with his hounds, after hunting, by a wicked woman.

'O where hae ye been, Lord Randal, my son?
O where hae ye been, my handsome young man?'—
'I hae been to the wild wood; mother, make my bed soon,
For I'm weary wi' hunting, and fain wald lie down.'

'Where gat ye your dinner, Lord Randal, my son?
Where gat ye your dinner, my handsome young man?'—
'I dined wi' my true love; mother, make my bed soon,
For I'm weary wi' hunting, and fain wald lie down.'

'What gat ye to your dinner, Lord Randal, my son?
What gat ye to your dinner, my handsome young man?'—
'I gat eels boil'd in broo'; mother, make my bed soon,
For I'm weary wi' hunting, and fain wald lie down.'

'What became of your bloodhounds, Lord Randal, my son?
What became of your bloodhounds, my handsome young man?'—

POEMS THAT TELL A STORY

'O they swell'd and they died; mother, make my bed soon,
For I'm weary wi' hunting, and fain wald lie down.'

'O I fear ye are poison'd, Lord Randal, my son!
O I fear ye are poison'd, my handsome young man!'—
'O yes! I am poison'd; mother, make my bed soon,
For I'm sick at the heart, and I fain wald lie down.'
(*Anon.*) (II. 49)

Then there is 'The Bonny Earl of Moray' (II. 112): 'Mary Hamilton' (II. 12)—this is one which should appeal particularly to girls: 'The Two Brethren' (I. 84), about two brothers, one of whom accidentally killed the other while they were ragging: 'Helen of Kirkconnell' (III. 83)—a very beautiful and dramatic poem: 'Young Hunting' (III. 99), which is really a sort of crime-story in verse, for it tells how a woman stabbed her lover to death, how she hid his body by putting it into a deep part of the Clyde, and how she was given away by her parrot which had witnessed the crime.

There are other ballads, such as 'The wee, wee man' (I. 3) and 'Thomas the Rhymer' (III. 144), which are about fairies and supernatural events. But even some of these (I imagine, though I cannot prove it) may be founded on fact. For example, 'Thomas the Rhymer' describes how a young poet was seized away from earth by a fairy and taken into fairyland, where he had to live for seven years: and this story might well have been made up to account for one of those mysterious disappearances—often due to loss of memory—which we read about in the newspapers today.

Some ballads, of course, are pure romance, pure fiction; but these are a small minority. The greatest of them, by far, is 'The Ancient Mariner' (III. 51). I expect most of you know it, so I'm not going to talk about it much here, except to point out two ways in which it differs from all the other ballads I've mentioned. First, we know who wrote it;—an English poet of the late eighteenth century called Coleridge: whereas the mass of ballads and folk-songs are by unknown, anonymous poets—'Anon.' is what you find under them instead of an author's name. The second point is this: the mass of ballads, as I told you, are stories written in verse; but 'The Ancient Mariner,' though the story in it is very thrilling indeed, is more than a story—it describes a mystical experience, and is almost a kind of parable. The mariner who shoots the albatross and brings bad luck and death to his shipmates, and is condemned to wander in uncharted seas, and finally is able to repent and be forgiven, symbolizes (that is, 'stands for') something in the human mind— the thing called conscience; and this great poem, like a parable, has a moral:

> He prayeth best, who loveth best
> All things both great and small;
> For the dear God who loveth us,
> He made and loveth all.

Poetry about people

Narrative poetry, like ballads, tells stories—sometimes pure fiction, but generally founded on fact: it uses, however, a greater variety of metres than the ballad. When a narrative poem is on a very big scale, like the 'Iliad' and 'Odyssey' of Homer, the 'Aeneid' of Virgil, or Milton's 'Paradise Lost' and 'Paradise Regained,' it is called an epic. The best narrative poetry in our language was written by Chaucer, who lived in the fourteenth century. His famous book, 'The Canterbury Tales,' is a collection of stories in verse, told by various members of a company of pilgrims with whom the poet is travelling to Canterbury. Chaucer was particularly interested in the way people looked and thought and behaved—an interest we associate nowadays much more with novelists than with poets.

If you take a giant's stride from Chaucer, across six centuries, you come to the present Poet Laureate, Mr. Masefield. Like Chaucer, he is interested in people and loves a good story. He has written a number of narrative poems, of the kind which boys and girls, as well as grown-ups, thoroughly enjoy, for they are written in simple language and are about things which any one can understand. He was a sailor himself for several years: his 'Salt Water Ballads' (I. 46 and 52) were some of the poems I myself first liked as a boy. Another English poet who was specially interested in people is Robert Browning. He lived in the latter part of the nineteenth century, at the same time as Tennyson. I expect many of you know Browning's poem, 'The Pied Piper of Hamelin' (I. 25); and that very dramatic one called 'My Last Duchess' you will enjoy too: both of them are excellent material for speaking aloud. Most of his poems about men and women, however, are a bit difficult to understand until you are grown-up and have had the kind of experiences yourself which he puts into them.

Tennyson's 'Ballad of the Revenge' (I. 7) I have mentioned before. Boys generally like stories about fighting. So, as well as 'The Revenge,' let me recommend to you 'Marmion' (II. 14), by Sir Walter Scott: it contains those thrilling lines:

> The stubborn spear-men still made good
> Their dark impenetrable wood,
> Each stepping where his comrade stood
> The instant that he fell.

POEMS THAT TELL A STORY

and Lord Macaulay's 'Lays of Ancient Rome,' which are brisk, spirited story-poems about the legendary heroes of Rome—Horatius Cocles, who held the bridge against great odds, is one of them. A special favourite of mine—and this is one which girls will like just as much as boys—is Jean Ingelow's 'The High Tide On The Coast of Lincolnshire' (II. 68): it is a narrative poem about a terrible tidal wave which swept inland in the year 1571, drowning herds and houses and people, but it is written in a more lyrical style than most such poems:

> . . . The heart had hardly time to beat,
> Before a shallow seething wave
> Sobbed in the grasses at our feet:
> The feet had hardly time to flee
> Before it brake against the knee,
> And all the world was in the sea.

There is one thing common to nearly all the poems I have mentioned in this chapter, and it is common to all story-poems. In such poetry, the *story* comes first. The poets could not have written these poems, of course, if their emotion had not been strongly stirred by the tales they had to tell. Their feelings, however, are subordinated to the story, giving it life and colour, but never pushing it into the background and taking the front of the stage themselves. In the next chapter we shall come to the kind of poems that are saturated with the poet's feelings and are written to express those feelings.

VI

MOODS, VISIONS AND SEASONS

The word 'lyric' has come to be used of any poetry which is not narrative or dramatic, satire or epigram. But it originally meant poetry that can be sung, and it's this kind of poetry I want to talk about first. The Elizabethans, as you know, loved music. Music was the regular thing at Court: friends would sit down after dinner to sing part-songs: there were musical instruments provided in barbers' shops, so that you could strum away while you waited to have your hair cut. Indeed, you weren't thought to be properly educated unless you could read musical notes as well as ordinary writing. At such a time, as you can imagine, the art of writing words for music, and music for words, flourished. The Elizabethan age was the first great period of the English lyric.

You may, for all that, be a bit disappointed at first when you begin to read Elizabethan lyrics. For one thing, they are so very often about love; and at your age people aren't generally much interested in love. Then, they will perhaps seem to you rather exaggerated and artificial in their idiom, or style. But, just because they are artificial, they are not necessarily insincere. In our ordinary, everyday speech we use slang and turns of phrase just as exaggerated, in their way, as the most flowery compliments of the Elizabethan poets: and we do it, as they did, simply because we are excited and like to splash about in words. They were also at the height of the Renaissance—the flood of classical learning and literature that was sweeping into England from the continent—which made them particularly interested in strict poetic *forms*. And besides, there was the influence of music: poems written for music, or under the influence of music, tend to be more artificial in diction than poems written simply to be read.

The best lyrics of this period for you to start with are the ones you find in Shakespeare's plays. Most of you know 'Come unto these yellow sands' (I. 18) and 'Where the bee sucks' (I. 99), 'Full fathom five, (I. 24) and 'Blow, blow, thou winter wind' (II. 10). You should certainly get to know, as well, 'Come away, Death' (III. 19), 'Take, oh take those lips away' (II. 56)—and the greatest of all—'Fear no more the heat o' the sun' (III. 26).

> Fear no more the heat o' the sun,
> Nor the furious winter's rages;
> Thou thy worldly task hast done,
> Home art gone, and ta'en thy wages;

Golden lads and girls all must,
As chimney-sweepers, come to dust.

Fear no more the frown o' the great,
Thou art past the tyrant's stroke:
Care no more to clothe and eat;   5
To thee the reed is as the oak:
The sceptre, learning, physic, must
All follow this, and come to dust.

Fear no more the lightning flash,
Nor the all dreaded thunder-stone;   10
Fear not slander, censure rash;
Thou hast finish'd joy and moan:
All lovers young, all lovers must
Consign to thee, and come to dust.

No exorciser harm thee!   15
Nor no witchcraft charm thee!
Ghost unlaid forbear thee!
Nothing ill come near thee!
Quiet consummation have;
And renownèd be thy grave.   20

(Shakespeare)

That poem is called a 'Dirge.' Yet, although it is about death, it is not really a sad poem. Why is this? Partly because it tells you that, once you are dead, you've nothing more to fear: but chiefly, I think, because the feeling behind it is that everything must come to an end sooner or later—golden lads, chimney sweepers, schoolmasters, chemists and kings—and there is nothing so very terrible about a natural process which happens to every one.

All those poems of Shakespeare were written to be sung: but they are also complete poems—they don't fade or collapse, as so many poems-for-music do, when you take the music away. From Shakespeare's songs, I suggest you should go on to such Elizabethan lyrics as Dekker's 'Lullaby' (I. 24), Campion's 'A Lamentation' (II. 3), Ben Jonson's 'Slow, slow, fresh fount' (II. 53), and Peel's 'His golden locks' (III. 38). If you can sing them or hear them sung, so much the better: but there is a music in the words themselves, which you will begin to hear if you say the poems aloud. In fact, poems that are actually set to music nearly always lose something of the *poetic* music which their words create; the notes of the music are apt to distort or cover up the beauty of the word-sounds.

How did the lyric become separated from music and turn into the wider thing we know as 'lyrical poetry'? I believe it was chiefly because poets began to see in the lyric a poetic form which could be used for wider, more varied purposes, to express a greater range and depth of meaning, provided they could cut it free from the artificial restraints imposed on it by music. Po-

etry, like the other arts—like the human race itself—
needs both tradition and experiment to keep it alive.
For poets, tradition is derived from the work of earlier
poets: certain rules for the writing of poetry are set
up by this work, certain laws governing both the spirit
and the form of poetry are established, and they are
handed down (tradition means a 'handing-down') to
later poets. But there comes a time when the poets
feel these rules to be oppressive: they have new things
to say, and the old forms seem to be more of a hindrance than a help. So the poets begin to break the
rules, to make experiments and create new forms, and
thus a kind of poetic revolution takes place. The new
forms they have invented, however, in their turn create
a tradition from which, in the course of time, later
poets will feel compelled to break away. Now, without a doubt, one of the biggest poetic revolutions that
has ever occurred was the separation of lyric poetry
from music.

A seamless garment

No revolution, however, completely breaks away
from the past. Wise rebels, while throwing aside
everything oppressive and worn-out which they have
inherited, try to take with them all the *good* things of
the past. The chief thing which poets took over from
the song-lyric and preserved in the new lyrical poetry

was—it's difficult to find exactly the right word for it, but let us call it 'singleness of mind.' A great writer once said of poetry that it should be 'simple, sensuous and passionate.' Let me try to explain what he meant by this. The imagination of the poet must be 'passionate,' at white heat, if it is to burn away all impurities in the poem, get rid of what is irrelevant or second-rate, and fuse his words into a single, shapely utterance. His senses must be all alive, so that he can feel things keenly and make the reader feel them through the 'sensuous' quality of the poem. An obvious example of this is Ben Jonson's poem, 'Have you seen but a bright lily grow.'

> Have you seen but a bright lily grow,
>   Before rude hands have touched it?
> Have you marked but the fall of the snow,
>   Before the soil hath smutched it?
>   Have you felt the wool of beaver,
>   Or swan's down ever?
>   Or have smelt o' the bud o' the briar
>   Or the nard i' the fire?
>   Or have tasted the bag o' the bee?
> O so white, O so soft, O so sweet is she!   (II. 24)

That is a very sensuous poem: the poet, by comparing his beloved with a lily, snow, swan's-down, briar-roses, honey, and so on, appeals to our senses (sight,

MOODS, VISIONS AND SEASONS 79

touch, smell, taste) much more successfully than if he had merely said, 'O so white, O so soft, O so sweet is she.'

The lyric poem, finally, must be 'simple.' This does not necessarily mean 'un-complex' or 'easy to understand'—some lyric poetry is highly complex and difficult. It means that the poem should convey a single mood, a single state of mind, and convey it in a form free from all irrelevances—a form which seems to have no 'joins' or patches, but fits the mood like a seamless coat.

Look out of your window the next night there is a full moon. Whether you are in town or country doesn't matter. The houses opposite, the familiar street, the lamp-posts; the fields and trees and gates: something has happened to them. Their outlines are still the same. But the moonlight has somehow made them both simpler and more mysterious: it has put a kind of glaze and glamour upon them, so that—instead of being a number of different, apparently unrelated objects—they have become parts of a single pattern. Lyric poetry has this effect of moonlight. It makes things at the same time simpler and more mysterious; it reveals patterns which we had not seen clearly before. And this capacity for simplifying was the gift that lyric poetry took over from the song-lyric. Songs were always, at heart, simple cries of joy or sorrow:

and love and death are still the two greatest themes of lyric poetry.

The surface of pure lyric poems is smooth as crystal. But crystal-gazers, staring into that innocent looking globe, begin to see shadows, figures moving, strange meanings.

> Take, oh take those lips away
> That so sweetly were forsworn,
> And those eyes, the break of day,
> Lights that do mislead the morn . . .

It looks so simple, at the first glance, doesn't it? But look at it again. If the 'eyes' Shakespeare is talking about *are* 'the break of day,' why do they '*mislead the morn*'? Yet—and this is the point—it is not necessary to understand the poem fully in order to be moved by it. We may have enjoyed a poem for years, before we have some experience in our own lives which gives us the clue to its full meaning. 'Still waters run deep,' the proverb says. Beneath the quiet, un-dramatic surface of thousands of lyric poems, there are depths of meaning—depths we shall never enter by worrying over the poem and pulling it to pieces.

A lyric poem is not necessarily bad, of course, if it has no such depth. 'Come unto these yellow sands'

and 'Where the bee sucks' are good poems, though in
effect they say no more than 'How jolly life is! Come
and enjoy it.' William Blake, many of whose visionary poems reveal layer after layer of meaning, also
wrote lyrics—'Songs of Innocence,' he called them—
which are the simplest expressions of joy or grief: for
instance, 'The Schoolboy' (I. 40) and 'The Echoing
Green' (I. 87). And the carols we sing at Christmas
or Easter are simple in the same way: they praise God;
they don't ask questions, or argue, or mean more than
they say.

Pure and simple

Most English lyrical poetry is not 'pure' in the sense
that those lyrics by Shakespeare and Blake are pure.
Purity is not the same thing as simplicity. Let us
compare two poems. The first is by Blake, the second
is a madrigal by an anonymous Elizabethan writer.

1. O rose, thou art sick!
    The invisible worm
    That flies in the night,
    In the howling storm,
    Has found out thy bed
    Of crimson joy;
    And his dark secret love
    Does thy life destroy.   (III. 107)

2. The silver swan who, living, had no note,
   When death approached, unlocked her silent throat:
   Leaning her breast against the reedy shore,
   Thus sang her first and last, and sang no more.
   Farewell all joys. O death, come, close mine eyes;
   More geese than swans now live, more fools than
      wise. (II. 96)

No one could call the Blake poem simple. It is more mysterious than the most difficult riddle I have ever been asked. But it sends a most violent feeling through me, like the shock of an electric current, even though I don't understand exactly what it means. The madrigal is calm, placid and perfectly simple by comparison: no riddles about it at all. Yet it is not *pure*, as the Blake poem is. Why not? Well, in the last two lines, through the mouth of the dying swan, the poet utters a *human opinion* about life. Obviously no swan, even if it was in the best of health, would be capable of thinking—let alone of saying, 'The world is going to the dogs. There are more geese than swans living, more fools than wise, so I really shan't be sorry to die.' The opinion about life implied in those two lines is an impurity—a foreign body, as it were, in the poem: and it is only the poet's skill which has managed to weave this opinion of his into the mood and texture of the poem without ruining its pattern. The Blake poem, on the other hand, contains no such impurity: although it can be interpreted in several different ways, at no point in it do you become aware of the poet breaking off his song to express a judgement, or weaving into his song a thought which has occurred to him.

The poet in contemplation

Though there are many passages of pure lyrical verse in English poetry, there are relatively few pure lyric poems. Most of what we call lyrical poetry should perhaps be called contemplative poetry. In this kind of verse the poet is not entirely merged into his subject: he seems to be standing from time to time a little apart from it, and meditating upon it: he tells us not only his feelings, but his thoughts, too. You can easily see the difference between these two kinds of poetry by comparing Thomas Hardy's 'This is the weather the cuckoo likes' with Wordsworth's poem, 'The Cuckoo.'

> This is the weather the cuckoo likes,
>   And so do I;
> When showers betumble the chestnut spikes,
>   And nestling fly:
> And the little brown nightingale bills his nest,
> And they sit outside at *The Travellers' Rest*,
> And maids come forth sprig-muslin drest,

And citizens dream of the south and west,
    And so do I.

This is the weather the shepherd shuns,
    And so do I;
When beeches drip in browns and duns,
    And thresh, and ply;
And hill-hid tides throb, throe on throe,
And meadow rivulets overflow,
And drops on gate-bars hang in a row,
And rooks in families homeward go,
    And so do I. (I. 90)

    O blithe New-comer! I have heard,
    I hear thee and rejoice.
    O Cuckoo! shall I call thee Bird,
    Or but a wandering voice?

    While I am lying on the grass
    Thy twofold shout I hear;
    From hill to hill it seems to pass
    At once far off, and near.

    Though babbling only to the Vale,
    Of sunshine and of flowers,
    Thou bringest unto me a tale
    Of visionary hours.

    Thrice welcome, darling of the spring!

MOODS, VISIONS AND SEASONS

Even yet thou art to me
No bird, but an invisible thing,
A voice, a mystery;

The same whom in my schoolboy days
I listened to; that Cry
Which made me look a thousand ways
In bush, and tree, and sky.

To seek thee did I often rove
Through woods and on the green;
And thou wert still a hope, a love;
Still longed for, never seen.

And I can listen to thee yet;
Can lie upon the plain
And listen, till I do beget
That golden time again.

O blessed Bird! the earth we pace
Again appears to be
An unsubstantial, faery place;
That is fit home for Thee!   (I. 54)

Hardy's poem (read it aloud to yourself) goes like a song; it gives you a series of pictures of summer and winter, but does not stop to meditate upon them; it tells you nothing about the poet himself, except that he likes being out-of-doors in the summer and indoors in the winter. Wordsworth's poem, on the other hand, tells you more about Wordsworth than it does about the cuckoo: the cuckoo is merely a symbol of the poet's mood, and its 'twofold shout' is, for him, a sort of open-sesame—a pass-word opening a door through which he can return to his boyhood days.

The first poetic form to be commonly used in England for contemplative verse came to us from Italy. It is called the sonnet. The poem of my own which I talked about on pages 44-49 is a sonnet. Sonnets are poems of fourteen lines, generally with five beats to each line; often the first eight lines state the theme, while the remaining six lines develop and finish it. There are certain fixed rhyme-schemes for the sonnet, too, from which—until recently—poets have very seldom broken away. Why it is, I don't know, but poets are particularly attracted to the sonnet form. It is an extremely difficult form, because it is not easy to compress into so small a space the kind of material which poets feel they want to put into it. But this act of compression, when the sonnet is successful, makes it extraordinarily rich in texture and in meaning. You have only to study Shakespeare's 'That time of year thou mayest in me behold' (III. 121), or Milton's 'When I consider how my light is spent' (III. 153), or Wordsworth's 'The world is too much with us' (III. 136) to see how closely thought and emotion can be woven into each other in the sonnet.

Poems about death

Another kind of contemplative poem in which our literature is particularly strong is the elegy. Elegies are not tied down to a single poetic form: but they share a common subject matter; they are all meditations upon death. Perhaps this sounds to you as if they must be very gloomy poems, and you may say that poets must be morbid to write them. But poets are, by their very nature, attracted to the mysterious, and death is a great mystery. Nor are elegies in fact gloomy. They are sad, in places at any rate, because they were inspired by the death of some one the poet loved. Yet they do not make *us* feel sad. When we read Milton's 'Lycidas', or Shelley's 'Adonais,' or Tennyson's 'In Memoriam', we realize that the poet has translated his own grief into something quite different: what started as a lament turns out to be almost a hymn of triumph: it is life—the beauty, wonder and majesty of life—that triumphs in these elegies, not death. Even when the poet has not yet reconciled himself to his friend's death, as Tennyson had not in 'In Memoriam' and Wilfrid Owen certainly had not in 'Futility' (III. 92), the emotion that he communicates to us through his poem is not pure grief or despair: it is the general emotion created by every work of art

—a feeling that we are in the presence of something greater than ourselves, something immortal: and it is also the special feeling which Vaughan put into words, writing of the dead—

> I see them walking in an air of glory
> Whose light doth trample on my days. . . .

Let us look at a passage from 'In Memoriam.' Tennyson has got over the first shock of his friend's death, and is remembering the garden and countryside in Lincolnshire where he himself spent his boyhood.

> Unwatch'd, the garden bough shall sway,
>   The tender blossom flutter down,
>   Unloved, that beech will gather brown,
> This maple burn itself away;
>
> Unloved, the sunflower, shining fair,
>   Ray round with flames her disk of seed,
>   And many a rose-carnation feed
> With summer spice the humming air;
>
> Unloved, by many a sandy bar,
>   The brook shall babble down the plain,
>   At noon or when the lesser wain
> Is twisting round the polar star;

Uncared for, gird the windy grove,
 And flood the haunts of hern and crake;
 Or into silver arrows break
The sailing moon in creek and cove;

Till from the garden and the wild
 A fresh association blow,
 And year by year the landscape grow
Familiar to the stranger's child;

As year by year the labourer tills
 His wonted glebe, or lops the glades;
 And year by year our memory fades
From all the circle of the hills.   (III. 148)

In the first four stanzas, Tennyson is saying, 'All the beautiful things I loved and admired in my young days —the blossoming trees, the sunflower and carnation, the brook and the water-birds—there was no one left to love and admire them after our childhood home was broken up.' Sorrow for his dead friend has changed into regret for the loved things of nature he has lost. But (this is the point) his regret for these things is not the strongest feeling the *reader* gets from the poem. It is the beauty and the glory of them that the reader chiefly feels. Sorrow has been turned into delight, even if the delight has a tinge of melancholy in it. And in the last two stanzas the poet recognizes the hard truth that beauty outlives all its worshippers: the landscape he loved in youthful days will 'grow familiar to the stranger's child'; the spirits of nature will live on for other hearts and eyes after the memory of his own people has faded 'from all the circle of the hills.'

'Ye Presences of Nature!'

The tradition of nature poetry—a tradition which goes back to the ancient belief that everything in nature contains a spirit—has continued strongly down to our own day. There is a great body of English poetry which has been created by the contemplation of nature. In this kind of poetry we don't usually get simple descriptions of natural scenes; nature is used, instead, as a background to the poet's thoughts and feelings, and as the impulse which sets them in motion. He finds, in nature, images which form and reflect a wider vision. He learns, as Blake said,

> To see a world in a grain of sand,
> And a heaven in a wild flower.
> (III. 141)

English poets as a whole (there were exceptions) up to the last years of the eighteenth century held what is called the 'classical' view of nature. When a Greek or Roman poet wrote about nature, he was

MOODS, VISIONS AND SEASONS

influenced by two things: his knowledge of its practical usefulness, and the folk-lore (as we should call it nowadays) which had grown up around his subject. The country, for him, was not—as it is for the modern town-dweller—a constellation of beauty spots; it was a living thing which had to be tamed and cultivated in order to provide man's food. The spirits of nature— the gods, goddesses, nymphs and satyrs—symbolized for him those forces which man had to conquer, or win over to his side and keep there, if he was to live a happy life. English poetry, at the Renaissance, took over this classical view of nature—and took over with it a whole gallery of gods and nymphs. The Elizabethan poets, for instance, *personified* the seasons of the year in the same way as did the Latin and Greek poets: the famous passage on the four seasons, from Spenser's 'The Faerie Queen' (III. 114), is an example of this. Even as far on as the early nineteenth century we find Keats, in his ode 'To Autumn' (II. 52), describing that season as a *person*—

> ... sitting careless on a granary floor,
> Thy hair soft-lifted by the winnowing wind;
> Or on a half-reaped furrow sound asleep,
> Drowsed with the fume of poppies ...

The danger of this personification of nature was that it tended to produce, after a while, artificial results, particularly when the poets didn't really believe that

these gods and nymphs existed, and only used them to
decorate their verse. Even today, when the classical
tradition is almost dead, we get people writing unreal,
coy, soppy little verses about gnomes, pixies, elfin
revels, and the like. The classical view was a good
influence, on the other hand, in so far as it impressed
on poets the essential usefulness and necessity of the
land.

One of the first important poets to break away from
the classical tradition was John Clare. 'Break away'
is hardly the right phrase, perhaps; for Clare was a
Northamptonshire ploughboy, and ploughboys didn't
get a classical education in 1800 any more than they
do today. Clare knew the land, of course, from practical experience, as a hard master. But he'd never
heard of the classical gods and nymphs. And out of
this combination of ignorance and experience, he created some of the loveliest nature poetry in our language. Much of it is *pure* nature poetry too, which
is a rare thing: it describes nature objectively; that is
to say, it leaves the poet's own feelings about it unspoken. Clare had a dazzling gift for observing things
and for finding the most illuminating words in which
to clothe his observations, as you can judge from lines
like—

The restless heat seems twittering by. (II. 37)

MOODS, VISIONS AND SEASONS

or, of the wagtail,

> And waddled in the water-pudge, and waggle went his tail,
> And chirrupt up his wings to dry upon the garden rail.

(I. 49)

or,

> While, far above, the solitary crane
> Swings lonely to unfrozen dykes again,
> Cranking a jarring melancholy cry
> Through the wild journey of the cheerless sky. (III. 136)

The sense of beauty

A vision is something which *you* see, or feel, and nobody else does. Blake was a visionary (some people called him a lunatic): he used to see angels. In a different way, Shelley was one. Wordsworth saw his visions through nature: he was a pantheist, which means—roughly speaking—that he believed everything in the universe to be part of God, and the *whole* of the universe to be the *whole* of God. In his greatest poem, 'The Prelude,' he describes how as a boy he grew to feel this sense of God in everything around him. 'The Prelude' as a whole is rather too difficult for you at your age. But it contains many passages which you will find interesting because they are about boyhood: for example, the one describing a skating expedition.

. . . And in the frosty season, when the sun
Was set, and visible for many a mile
The cottage windows blazed through twilight gloom,
I heeded not their summons: happy time
It was indeed for all of us—for me
It was a time of rapture! Clear and loud
The village clock tolled six,—I wheeled about,
Proud and exulting like an untired horse
That cares not for his home. All shod with steel,
We hissed along the polished ice in games
Confederate, imitative of the chase
And woodland pleasures,—the resounding horn,
The pack loud chiming, and the hunted hare.
So through the darkness and the cold we flew,
And not a voice was idle; with the din
Smitten, the precipices rang aloud;
The leafless trees and every icy crag
Tinkled like iron; while far distant hills
Into the tumult sent an alien sound
Of melancholy not unnoticed, while the stars
Eastward were sparkling clear, and in the west
The orange sky of evening died away.
Not seldom from the uproar I retired
Into a silent bay, or sportively
Glanced sideway, leaving the tumultuous throng,
To cut across the reflex of a star
That fled, and, flying still before me, gleamed
Upon the glassy plain; and oftentimes,
When we had given our bodies to the wind,

And all the shadowy banks on either side
Came sweeping through the darkness, spinning still
The rapid line of motion, then at once
Have I, reclining back upon my heels,
Stopped short; yet still the solitary cliffs
Wheeled by me—even as if the earth had rolled
With visible motion her diurnal round!
Behind me did they stretch in solemn train,
Feebler and feebler, and I stood and watched
Till all was tranquil as a dreamless sleep.
              (*Wordsworth*) (III. 9)

Compare that with 'Midnight Skaters' by a living poet, Edmund Blunden.

> The hop-poles stand in cones,
>   The icy pond lurks under,
> The pole-tops steeple to the thrones
>   Of stars, sound gulfs of wonder;
> But not the tallest there, 'tis said,
> Could fathom to this pond's black bed.
>
>
> Then is not death at watch
>   Within those secret waters?
> What wants he but to catch
>   Earth's heedless sons and daughters?
> With but a crystal parapet
> Between, he has his engines set.

> Then on, blood shouts, on, on,
>   Twirl, wheel and whip above him,
> Dance on this ball-floor thin and wan,
>   Use him as though you love him;
> Court him, elude him, reel and pass,
> And let him hate you through the glass.   (II. 57)

Both the Wordsworth and the Blunden poems have a visionary touch. On the surface, they are concerned with the exhilaration of skating. But neither of them is *just* a poem about skating. Blunden sees, beneath the surface of the ice, death lurking: the thinner the ice, the more exciting it is to skate on it. The poem could be taken as a parable—'in the midst of life we are in death.' Wordsworth's vision is of Life. He makes us aware of nature in the background—the hills, the stars, the wind and the darkness—as a living presence neither friendly nor hostile to the skaters, but containing a power and a wisdom of its own which human beings can draw upon if they wish. After the Wordsworth passage quoted above, there come the famous lines—

> Ye Presences of Nature in the sky
> And on the earth! Ye Visions of the hills!
> And Souls of lonely places! . . .

Long contemplation of nature only confirmed for

Wordsworth what he had felt as a boy—what you and I and all of us feel when we allow nature to take possession of us—that a mysterious power is speaking to us through it. We may try to put it into words by talking about 'the beauty of nature.' But the phrase doesn't get us very far. After all, it's not only nature —earth, sea or sky—which gives us this sense of beauty; we can get it from man-made things—towns, factories, ships, trains, aeroplanes: which seems to suggest that beauty is, as the proverb says, 'in the eye (it should be, 'in the imagination') of the beholder.'

The meditation of nature's beauty, which we find in Wordsworth's poetry, in Keats' and Shelley's, often in the poetry of Tennyson, in Arnold's 'Thyrsis' (II. 25) and 'Scholar Gipsy,' in Thomas Hardy and many later poets, is—in this strict sense of contemplating it for its own sake or for the truth it may tell us—quite a modern thing. It may, perhaps, be connected with the rise of urban civilization. As people came to live more and more in towns, they lost their sense of the practical use of the country. (I've heard of city-bred children today who genuinely believed that milk comes out of a bottle and had no idea it must come out of a cow first.) But, although his *practical* link with nature is broken, the townsman still has an *instinctive feeling* for the land, inherited from thousands of ancestors who lived on it: and it is this instinct which gives him a mysterious feeling of sympathy with nature—a feeling which his spokesman, the poet, puts into words.

VII

POETRY WITH A PURPOSE

Of course, all poetry-writing has a purpose: and this purpose, as you have discovered by now, is to create out of the poet's experience and skill a poem with a life of its own—a thing perfect in itself, as a daffodil is perfect in itself (in a way, to ask what is the 'meaning' of a poem is as unnecessary as to ask what is the meaning of a daffodil). But what I'm going to talk about in this chapter is poetry of various kinds which, beside the poetic purpose, has some other purpose as well. There is an enormous field of this dual-purpose poetry, ranging from the plays of Shakespeare to the inscriptions on tombstones, from limericks to the satires of Pope, from sea-shanties to hymns. The dividing line between poetry and poetry-with-a-purpose is, in practice, almost impossible to define: and there is a great deal of English verse of which it is difficult to say whether it falls on the one side of the line or the other: often we come across a poem, for instance, whose main object seems at first to be to teach the reader some lesson—a poem with a moral: but then, in the middle of it, the poet forgets he is supposed to be teaching you something, and bursts into song just like a lyric poet.

You may be surprised to find that I have put Shakespeare's plays into this class. It is quite true, of course, that they contain some of the very greatest and wisest poetry ever written: at any moment we may find Shakespeare apparently forgetting his job, which was to get on with the play, and holding up the action in order to release through the mouth of one of the characters a flood of that pure poetry with which his imagination brimmed over. But, if we look harder at these poetic passages in his plays, we generally find they are not just there for fun: they have a dramatic purpose too; they tell us something about the characters, or about the theme of the play as a whole; they are, in themselves, dramatic crises and highlights.

This is true of all good poetic drama, and is the difference between it and the dramatic verse we find in ballads and narrative poems. In the latter, the poet is concerned to compose verse which will tell his story in the most stirring manner possible. In poetic drama, the poet has many other things to think of—problems of stage technique which he must solve if the play is to be a success. Successful poetic drama, in fact, subordinates the poetry to the drama. Shakespeare, Marlowe, Webster and the many other dramatists who flourished between 1580 and 1640 worked in close co-operation with producers and actors; and their plays were popular, not chiefly because they were written in verse (though the audiences of those days did enjoy poetry on the stage), but because these poets knew their job as dramatists and made their verse serve the purposes of the theatre. For this reason, it is much easier both to enjoy and to understand Shakespeare's plays by seeing them in the theatre, or acting them yourselves, than by reading them out of a book.

'Teach me, my God and King'

The seventeenth century, that saw the decline of poetic drama, was particularly rich, however, in another kind of poetry—in religious verse. A religious poem may do one, or both, of two things. It may glorify God, or it may try to teach us a moral lesson— a lesson about right and wrong. As far back as the Middle Ages there had been a strong tradition in England linking Christianity with literature. There were Nativity Plays and Miracle Plays, whose subjects—episodes from the Bible—were treated with a remarkable blend of reverence, free imagination and humour. There were Morality Plays, in which the virtues and vices were personified, just as the forces of nature are personified in much early nature-poetry. Beside plays, there were the religious songs we call 'carols.' These are simple, lively productions, written to old folk-tunes, and they sometimes reach considerable poetic heights. 'As Joseph was a-walking' (I. 5), for instance, and 'There comes a ship a-sailing' (I. 71) and 'Here we bring new water' (III. 37), and that loveliest of all carols, 'I sing of a maiden,' are full of poetic imagination.

> I sing of a maiden
>   That is makèless;
> King of all kings
>   To her son she ches.
>
> He came all so still
>   Where his mother was,
> As dew in April
>   That falleth on the grass.
>
> He came all so still
>   To his mother's bower,
> As dew in April
>   That falleth on the flower.
>
> He came all so still
>   Where his mother lay,
> As dew in April
>   That falleth on the spray.
>
> Mother and maiden
>   Was never none but she;

> Well may such a lady
> Godès mother be.
>
> *(Anon.)* (II. 33)

In the seventeenth century the lyric stream of religious verse broadened and deepened. The greatest poet of this time—and he is the greatest religious poet in England's history—was John Milton. He was a Puritan. His best-known work, 'Paradise Lost' (III. 6), is a kind of epic in which God and Satan instead of an Achilles and a Hector are the antagonists; in which there is a battle—not between human warriors as in Homer's epic, but between ideas of good and evil. Andrew Marvell, another Puritan, wrote poetry that seems surprisingly coloured and sensuous for a Puritan to have composed (II. 109; III. 151 and 159).

'A winged sentry'

But the best religious poetry of this time was not all written by Puritans. Herbert and Vaughan were Anglicans; Crashaw became a Roman Catholic: their religious poems, particularly Crashaw's, often sound like love poems, which happen to be addressed to Christ or the saints and not to a woman.

One of my favourite poems of this period is Herbert's 'Virtue':

> Sweet day, so cool, so calm, so bright,

> The bridal of the earth and sky,
> The dew shall weep thy fall to-night;
> > For thou must die.
>
> Sweet rose, whose hue angry and brave
> Bids the rash gazer wipe his eye,
> Thy root is ever in its grave,
> > And thou must die
>
> Sweet spring, full of sweet days and roses,
> A box where sweets compacted lie,
> My music shows ye have your closes,
> > And all must die.
>
> Only a sweet and virtuous soul,
> Like season'd timber, never gives;
> But though the whole world turn to coal,
> > Then chiefly lives.

That does not sound like a religious poem at the start, does it? In fact, it is not till the last stanza that we are made aware of the poem's purpose. All sweet and beautiful things must die, the poet has been saying: but goodness, the soul of a good man, does not die—'Only a sweet and virtuous soul, Like seasoned timber, never gives.' The object of Herbert's poem, then, is to teach us (through beauty) a moral lesson. Vaughan's 'Peace,' another great favourite of mine, so simple and bold in its language, so confident in the belief it expresses, though it has a moral, is a good example of the other kind of religious poetry, whose purpose is to glorify God:

> My soul, there is a country
>   Far beyond the stars,
> Where stands a winged sentry
>   All skilful in the wars:
>
> There, above noise and danger,
>   Sweet peace sits crowned with smiles,
> And One born in a manger
>   Commands the beauteous files.
>
> He is thy gracious friend,
>   And—O my soul, awake!—
> Did in pure love descend,
>   To die here for thy sake.
>
> If thou canst get but thither,
>   There grows the flower of peace,
> The Rose that cannot wither,
>   Thy fortress and thy ease.
>
> Leave then thy foolish ranges,
>   For none can thee secure
> But One, who never changes,
>   Thy God, thy life, thy cure. (III. 94)

So, you see, a religious poem does not have to be dimly 'pious' or colourless or forbidding. In fact, the best religious poetry never is: even a good hymn never is, as you will see if you look at Cowper's 'God moves in a mysterious way,' (III. 27) or Watts' 'Our God, our help in ages past' (II. 47).

We should not think of religious poetry as in a different class from other poetry. The religious experience—a divine vision, a passionate faith in God—may, like any other intense experience, create poetry. But, in so far as the poet has put his powers at the service of a religious belief or is urging upon us some moral lesson, his verse may conveniently come under the heading of 'poetry-with-a-purpose,' and that is why I have mentioned it in this chapter.

Poems of hate

'*Poems* of hate?' you're asking: 'but surely hatred is something barren and destructive?' Not where poetry is concerned. Any strong emotion can produce poetry. Love of God can produce it, and so can hatred of a man. You can hate another man for personal reasons—because you don't like his character, or his manners, or his face, or the way he has treated you: or you can hate him because you believe his ideas to be wicked. Poetry which attacks people, or attacks the political, religious, or social ideas they hold, is called

POETRY WITH A PURPOSE

'satire' (satire can be written in prose too, but the verse form gives it a sharper edge). The keenest weapon of satire is laughter: if you can make your opponent look ridiculous it's as good as a knock-out: the greatest master of this weapon, in the English language, is a poet called Alexander Pope, who lived in the eighteenth century. Here, for example, is what he wrote about Lord Hervey, a nobleman who had insulted him.

> Yet let me flap this bug with gilded wings,
> This painted child of dirt that stinks and stings;
> Whose buzz the witty and the fair annoys,
> Yet wit ne'er tastes, and beauty ne'er enjoys. . . .
> Eternal smiles his emptiness betray,
> As shallow streams run dimpling all the way.
> Whether in florid impotence he speaks,
> And, as the prompter breathes, the puppet squeaks:
> Or at the ear of Eve, familiar toad,
> Half froth, half venom, spits himself abroad. . . .

It's a wonder that Lord Hervey was ever able to hold up his head again. Another poem by Pope that will amuse you is the one in which he makes fun of a vulgar millionaire whom he calls 'Timon.' There had been plenty of hate-poetry in the English language before the eighteenth century. But the great age of English satire began with Dryden, who flourished at the end of seventeenth century, and ended with Byron at the beginning of the nineteenth.

The prevailing tone of eighteenth-century verse is summed up in Pope's line, 'The proper study of mankind is man.' The poetry of this period was formal and witty. It was for the most part a poetry of moral and political ideas. This was not the first time, of course, that poets had used their verse for the expression of such ideas. But never before had they been so closely connected with political parties. In the eighteenth century, many writers were hired by Whig or Tory politicians, to put over the principles of their own party and attack those of their opponents. Apart from the great writers, like Dryden, Pope and Swift, there was a whole mob of literary gangsters, who went for each other tooth-and-nail, using words instead of tommy guns. It was a lively period, and you had to be pretty tough to stand up against the volleys of satire that were fired off at you, both in prose and in verse.

Political verse is an obvious example of poetry-with-a-purpose. Nowadays we should call it propaganda—though nowadays, since the libel law is so much stricter, writers in England dare not attack their enemies with the violence and unscrupulousness of the eighteenth century. But once again, the fact that this kind of verse has a purpose—the fact that it is aimed to affirm one set of ideas or discredit another—does not make it inferior poetry. It all depends on whether the poet has *felt* these ideas intensely and thus passed them through the furnace of the poetic imagination. Political verse is, of course, not necessarily satire. There are great political sonnets by Milton and Wordsworth, for example, which speak out for liberty with a noble and positive voice. The theme of liberty has always inspired poets, from the greatest down to the unknown writers of political ballads such as 'The Wearing of the Green' (II. 44).

The Iron Duke and Billy Brown

Another kind of poetry-with-a-purpose is called 'occasional poetry,' which means poetry written for some special occasion. If a friend of his got married, a poet might write an 'epithalamium,' or wedding poem: if a friend died, he might compose an 'epitaph' —a short inscription in verse to be put on his tomb. He would send him an ode on his birthday, or a poem of farewell if the friend was going abroad. One seventeenth-century poet even wrote a poem to celebrate the occasion when his patron caught the small-pox: as he relied on his patron for a living, the poem had somehow to be a flattering one, but he went a bit far in comparing the small-pox spots to pearls. Occasional poetry sounds as if, being more or less written to order, it must be rather uninspired. But this is not necessarily so. For instance, when Tennyson was Poet Laureate (until recently, it was held the duty of the Poet Laureate to commemorate public events) he wrote an ode on the death of the Duke of Wellington, which is one of his finest poems.

> Where shall we lay the man whom we deplore?
> Here, in streaming London's central roar.
> Let the sound of those he wrought for,
> And the feet of those he fought for,
> Echo round his bones for evermore.

Then there is a kind of didactic (or 'teaching') poetry which has a quite practical purpose. Two great poets, one Greek and one Latin, each wrote a verse text-book on farming: these books gave the most useful advice on how to cultivate the land and look after live-stock (one of them was written partly in order to persuade people to go back on to the land), but they also rise at times to real heights of poetry. There was an English poet of the eighteenth century who wrote a long poem on the growing of cider apples and the making of cider. And even today, in the London underground railways, we find little pieces of verse about a certain 'Billy Brown of London town'—verse whose purpose is to teach travellers how to behave sensibly in the Tube.

POETRY WITH A PURPOSE

Finally, I should mention song-poems composed as an actual accompaniment to work. You may have heard some Hebridean songs on the radio: many of these were composed by the Hebrideans, both words and tunes, to help them when they were rowing their boats or weaving their cloth; and, if you go to the Outer Hebrides, you can still hear them sung for this practical purpose today. The songs we call 'sea-shanties' (I. 15: II. 102) had the same object. These shanties (or 'chanties') were made up by seamen in the days of sailing ships, when all the work was done by hand, to be sung *in time with* the various rhythms of work on board ship—hauling on ropes, turning the capstan, and so on. There are brisk ones like 'What shall we do with the drunken sailor,' and beautiful melancholy ones like 'Shenandoah' or 'Lowlands away' (III. 90).

VIII

POEMS OF YESTERDAY AND TODAY

The last three chapters will have given you some idea of the great variety there is in poetry, of the many uses to which it has been put. It has been used to tell stories, to convey moral lessons, scientific ideas or practical knowledge; to praise God; to attack one's enemies; to make people laugh, to make them work or fight better; to be sung; to be spoken in the theatre; to celebrate public events; and to communicate the poet's private experience. Now the first thing we notice when we look at modern English poetry poetry written during the last forty years or so—is that almost all the uses of poetry except the last seem to have disappeared. Only a few story poems have been written, a certain amount of political verse, a little Christian poetry; hardly any satire, hardly any poetic drama; the tradition of good occasional verse has been lost; scientific or moral ideas (though they often colour modern verse) are not systematically presented in it. The poetry of belief, of knowledge or instruction has given way almost entirely to the poetry of feeling.

Some people think this is a good thing. It was never poetry's proper job, they argue, to instruct you,

to put over ideas, or even simply to entertain you.
Writers originally used poetry for these purposes because verse is easier to memorize than prose, and in
the days when books were very scarce it was necessary
to present knowledge in a concise and memorable
form. Nowadays, these people say, you have cheap
books, radio, newspapers, cinemas to instruct and
entertain you, and poetry can settle down to its real
job—the task of creating out of words and the poet's
experience a special kind of world, quite separate from
the ordinary everyday world, yet illuminating it and
making you more aware of its inner nature.

Now I myself partly agree with this point of view.
I certainly think the highest function of poetry is not
to impart knowledge or persuade you that certain
things are right or wrong, but to sharpen your senses
and to give you a special kind of wisdom—the kind
that comes from exercising your imagination. On the
other hand, it's not true to say that only 'pure' poetry
can do this. Every poem—not only a lyric or contemplative poem, but a ballad or a satire, or a description of pruning apple-trees or flying an aircraft—will,
provided it's a *good* poem, create a little world of its
own and light up our imagination. Moreover, if we
say that the chief job of poetry isn't to entertain us, or
help us to pass exams, or make us better citizens, it
becomes extremely difficult to convince some people

that there's any point in poetry at all. We have to fall back on vague phrases like 'exercising the imagination,' 'enriching our spiritual lives,' 'making us more aware of the world,' and so on; and such phrases don't mean much to the ordinary man.

When I was talking about poetry at a school one day, a boy—he is going to be an engineer and is, quite rightly, sceptical about vague ideas—asked me, 'What would happen supposing poetry stopped tomorrow?' It was a shrewd question. At the time, I gave him the answer he obviously wanted: 'Nothing at all would happen, the world would go on just the same.' Now I've had time to think about it, I'd like to put that answer a bit differently. You see, it's almost impossible that people will ever stop writing poetry. Even today, when poetry has become the Cinderella of the Arts, when poets make scarcely any money out of their verse and only get fame within a small circle of readers, just as many people are writing it as ever. The poet may seem to have lost his audience, but he still goes on writing because, for some people, poetry is the natural way of expressing themselves. Even if every one stopped reading or listening to poetry (and as a matter of fact the B.B.C. have discovered that the audience for their poetry readings is seldom less than 300,000 listeners, and often as high as a million), there would still be poets writing it. So poetry *can't* stop. The budding engineer who asked me that question might just as well have asked, 'What would happen supposing iron stopped tomorrow?' The answer is, 'But it won't.' And, though one day all the iron deposits in the earth may be exhausted, the engineer will find some other material to build his bridges with. Whereas the poet's material—words—is inexhaustible; so he can go on building his poetic bridges till kingdom come.

Bridges into the unknown

A living American poet, Robert Frost, has said that a poem 'begins in delight and ends in wisdom.' This is true both for the poet and the reader. The poet starts to compose a poem because the joy of creation has seized him: and, as the poem takes shape, his own ideas and feelings become more clearly defined. He does not take a truth and write about it. What happens is that, in the process of writing (if the poem is successful), some unguessed or dimly-perceived truth grows clearer to him. Just the same with the reader. He 'begins in delight,' begins by enjoying the poem for its beautiful sounds, images and associations: but, after a while, he finds that, through the enjoyment, some truth has entered his mind and he has become wiser.

This is the real, final answer to those who claim that

today poetry is obsolete, or at best a sort of jam on the plain bread-and-butter of life—pleasant, but not necessary. Every good poem, in fact, is a bridge built from the known, familiar side of life over into the unknown. Science, too, is always making expeditions into the unknown. But this does not mean that science can supersede poetry. For poetry enlightens us in a different way from science: it speaks directly to our feelings and our imagination. The findings of poetry are no more and no less true than those of science. To go back to the rainbow I mentioned in the first chapter: science tells us the *facts* behind the rainbow—refraction and reflection of the sun's rays in drops of rain; poetry starts from our *feelings* when we see a rainbow, and makes a bridge or link between them and our feelings about other things. We cannot think poetry unimportant unless we think our feelings are unimportant.

In Christmas crackers one used sometimes to find sheets of paper sprinkled over with numbered dots. The dots didn't seem to make any recognizable pattern. But, if you took a pencil and drew lines from one dot to another, in the order in which they were numbered, you found when you came to the last dot you had drawn a cow or a ship or some other quite familiar thing. All through life, but particularly when we are young, the things that happen to us and our feelings about them often seem as meaningless and unconnected as the dots on those cracker papers. What poetry does is to draw the lines, make the bridges, from point to point in our experience, and thus reveal the pattern they form. This indeed is poetry's great gift to man—the revealing to him that every human experience, instead of being isolated or meaningless, is part of an intelligible pattern.

Modern myths

Primitive poets created myths to represent the mysterious workings of nature, or legends in which the deeds of men were immortalized. Many modern poets have occupied themselves with another field— the workings of man's mind. Now this is a field hitherto comparatively little explored by science or poetry. The science of psychology is still at an experimental stage: but it has discovered enough to suggest that there is a large part of our mind (it calls this 'the unconscious mind') about which we know very little, but which has a great influence in shaping our conscious thoughts and our actions. Here is an example. Man used to believe that dreams were prophetic, and try to interpret them as symbolic of future events: you remember Joseph and Pharaoh's dreams in the Bible? Some modern psychologists, on the other hand, believe that dreams are thrown up by our unconscious mind; that they represent desires, memories, fears, anxieties which, for one reason or another, are prevented from coming up into our conscious mind; and by studying a patient's dreams, and discovering what their weird symbols represent for him, a psychologist can help to free the patient from mental difficulties which were making him unhappy. Throughout the ages, poets have been fascinated by dreams and visions. Today, some of them are exploring this region of the unconscious, creating myths, not of man's battles with nature or other men, but of the hidden forces which, like sea-monsters, move and struggle beneath the surface of his mind.

Another field of material which has been opened to modern poets is that of machinery. Within a period of about a hundred and fifty years, as you know, civilization has been revolutionized by machines. At first, the poets resented these machines, and either ignored them altogether in their poetry or took up a hostile attitude towards them: Blake, for instance, wrote of the 'dark Satanic mills,' and any one who has read about the appalling conditions in mine and factory during the Industrial Revolution will understand his anger. The first important English poet to write sympathetically about machines was Kipling, who at times seems to admire them more than he admires human beings: notice how he personifies machines, attributing to them human virtues and vices as did the primitive poets to the forces of nature.

In the 1930's a sustained effort was made by some poets to create myths out of the machine-age in which we live, and to use modern inventions in their poetry. They have been criticized for doing this, mainly on two grounds—(*a*) that machines are ugly, and poetry ought to be concerned only with the beautiful; (*b*) that, to be so taken up with machines, implies a loss of faith in humanity. The second criticism is the stronger of the two: but at a period when humanity seemed to have failed abjectly in finding any solution to the problems of unemployment and want, or any answer to the threat of war, these poets were speaking as prophets, warning mankind that, if it did not make a right use of its own inventions, it would be enslaved and destroyed by them. With regard to the first criticism, most poets today would reply, I think, that machines are not ugly and that in any case poetry is not necessarily concerned with what is generally accepted as 'beautiful.'

Factories and sunsets

If you are profoundly excited by the roaring power of an express engine, or the grace of an aircraft in flight, or the complex din and movement of a factory, you may produce good poetry out of them as naturally as earlier poets could produce it out of a storm, a sunset or a bird. The real difficulty about absorbing into verse the products of the machine age and of city life is that they have not yet the same wealth of association as is attached to nature or the products of rural civilization. *Potentially*, they are quite as 'romantic': just think how much romance there is in those everyday objects, telegraph poles, for instance.

A third great modern myth is being formed, which is closely related to the machine-myth. The invention of all these machines has given mankind, for the first time in recorded history, the chance of material plenty for *all*. We have the means today to produce enough food, clothing and other material necessities of life for every one in the world. Yet, even before the war, millions of people were not getting them. The practical solution of this problem lies, of course, within the field of politics and economics. But, during the last fifteen years, many poets approached it too from the standpoint of the 'social conscience.' They wished to exercise the poet's ancient right to speak on behalf of the community, and to say, 'It is a wicked thing that men should starve in a world of plenty: it goes against the conscience of a civilized society, and society should not tolerate it.' In doing so, they produced a good deal of political verse which, because it talked of things that came within most people's experience, won a certain popularity.

A language always changing

Modern poets, then, have been trying to extend the field of poetry, to bring into their poetry ideas and objects which had not received poetic treatment before. Not only the subject-matter, but the language of poetry has been changing too. It always is changing, of course: every poet has to find his own voice—he can't be satisfied with clever imitations of other poets' styles—and in finding it he influences to a greater or lesser degree the whole poetic language of his time. In a century like our own, which has seen so many and rapid changes in the outside world, it was inevitable that there should be poetic revolutions as well. You cannot put new wine into old bottles, and you cannot put new ideas, new images into the old poetic idioms.

For this reason, many older people find modern poetry obscure. Younger people, if they are interested in poetry at all, do not have nearly so much difficulty with it: they have not read so much of the older poets as to prevent them understanding the language of the newer ones; and they are naturally prejudiced in favour of poetry which seems to be talking about up-to-date, interesting things. But remember that, where poetry is concerned, being up-to-date is not at all important. A poem will not survive unless it is good in itself, and it isn't good just because it brings in aeroplanes or Einstein's theory. Much of the best poetry of our century—the poetry of Hardy and Yeats, of Housman, Bridges and de la Mare, of Wilfrid Owen, Robert Frost and Edward Thomas— may already seem, to people of your generation, old-fashioned. Well, Shakespeare seemed old-fashioned to a number of eighteenth-century critics. That was their mistake, and their loss.

IX

WHEN IS A POEM NOT A POEM?

The reason why one poem excites us, while another leaves us cold, is very difficult to discover. A poem may obey all the rules, be flawless in technique, yet we may find it as magnificently lifeless as an empty mansion. Another poem may be careless in execution, or lack the airs and graces of poetry, and yet our imagination responds to it. I do not mean to suggest that, because you are stirred by a poem, it is necessarily a good one: millions of people have been profoundly moved by the hymn 'Abide with me,' which is really not good verse at all. And yet, although the emotion it rouses in us is not an absolute test of a poem's quality, it is certainly the first test. Many poets and critics have given evidence of the almost physical effect which great poetry has upon them: A. E. Housman said that, if certain lines of poetry came into his head when he was shaving, they made his hair bristle so stiffly that the razor couldn't cut it. Unless you are first thrilled by a poem, it's not likely that you will be able to make any fair criticism of it or to comprehend fully its meaning (for the 'meaning,' remember, reaches you *through* the emotional effect the poem has upon you).

Now I'm going to assume that all of you who are reading this book do in fact enjoy *some* poetry. If there is only one poem in the world you really like, you are on the way to enjoying a great many more poems. How, then, do you reach the next stage— the stage of deciding whether a poem is a good one, or which of two poems you enjoy is the better? Let's try a test. Underneath, you will find two poems printed. Read them aloud to yourself: try to *feel* them: let the words blow over you like a wind. Then, without reading any further, say which is the better poem.

(A) As I was going down Treak Street
 For half a pound of treacle,
 Who should I meet but my old friend Micky Thumps
 He said to me, 'Wilt thou come to our wake?'
 I thought a bit,
 I thought a bit,
 I said I didn't mind:
 So I went.

 As I was sitting on our doorstep
 Who should come by but my old friend Micky Thumps' brother.
 He said to me, 'Wilt thou come to our house?
 Micky is ill.'
 I thought a bit,

I thought a bit,
I said I didn't mind:
So I went.

And he were ill:
He were gradely ill.
He said to me,
'Wilt thou come to my funeral, mon, if I die?'
I thought a bit,
I thought a bit,
I said I didn't mind:
So I went.

And it *were* a funeral.
Some stamped on his grave:
Some spat on his grave:
But I scraped my eyes out for my old friend Micky Thumps.

And here is the second poem:

(B) Man proposes, God in His time disposes,
And so I wandered up to where you lay,
A little rose among the little roses,
And no more dead than they.

It seemed your childish feet were tired of straying,
You did not greet me from your flower-strewn bed,
Yet still I knew that you were only playing—
Playing at being dead.

> I might have thought that you were really sleeping,
> So quiet lay your eyelids to the sky.
> So still your hair, but surely you were peeping,
> And so I did not cry.
>
> God knows, and in His proper time disposes,
> And so I smiled and gently called your name,
> Added my rose to your sweet heap of roses,
> And left you to your game.

True feeling and false

Well, have you made up your mind? Perhaps you have decided that this second poem is the better one. 'Of course it is,' some of you are saying: 'it rhymes, and it has a clear metre; besides, the language is so much more poetical—it talks about roses, which are poetical, while the other poem starts off with half a pound of treacle, which isn't.' And, when I tell you that the second poem was written by a professional poet well-known in his day, while the first is by an anonymous Lancashire ballad writer, you may be still more convinced that B is the better poem.

But you will be quite wrong. I believe any experienced judge of poetry would agree with me that A is in a higher class altogether than B, as far as two poems so different in style can be compared (they are easy to compare in another way, because they both have the same subject—the death of a loved person).

WHEN IS A POEM NOT A POEM?

I'll tell you why I think A is better. It has none of the things we normally associate with poetry, I admit: no rhyme or fixed metre, no simile or epithets, not a single metaphor. But it has what is more important than all these—a most passionate feeling, which creates poetry out of the simple words, the prosaic expressions it uses. Notice the tragic irony of the story it tells. First, Micky Thumps invites the writer to his wake (holiday party): then Micky Thumps' brother invites him to the house, because Micky has fallen ill: then Micky invites him to his own funeral. Notice how effectively the refrain is used; how the understatement of 'I thought a bit, I said I didn't mind, So I went' throws into relief the mounting tragic excitement of the poem. And then, in the last four lines, how vivid and violent and *real* is the little scene at the funeral! The savage phrase, 'I scraped my eyes out,' tells us more than whole books could about the writer's passionate grief for his old friend Micky Thumps. This poem is a true ballad, a story whose dry bones are brought to life by the strength of the writer's emotion.

Poem B is graceful, charming and musical; but it does not move me at all, while the first poem does: there is something shallow and false about the feeling in it. At a first reading, the poet's fancy that the dead child is not really dead, but is only 'playing at being dead,' may seem to you rather a pretty one. But, when we think a bit more, we find it's not at all satisfactory. Why not? Because it isn't true. For me, at any rate, the whole poem is falsified by the fact that the child *is* dead and the poet is playing a sort of make-believe game with it. Death is such a big thing that it makes any pretence look rather silly. So fancies like 'you were only playing' and 'surely you were peeping' and 'left you to your game' don't seem to ring true. These criticisms could be summed up by saying that the poem is 'sentimental.' Sentimentality is sentiment (or feeling) which has somehow gone bad: when feeling goes bad, it turns either sour or oversweet: the feeling in this poem is, to my taste, oversweet.

How to judge a poem

Sentimentality is one of the first things to watch out for, when you are criticizing a poem. This is because, as I've said before, the first test of a poem is whether it thrills you: and, until we have developed a keen sense of taste, we are likely to be thrilled just as much (or more) by the sentimental as by true sentiment. This applies to music, novels, painting, the cinema, too. Up to a point, even the young reader can distinguish for himself between true and false feeling. It's a matter of asking yourself, when the first excitement of a new poem has passed, 'Does the poem really

WHEN IS A POEM NOT A POEM?

ring true? Is the feeling in it genuine, or has it been faked up?' But there's not the least need to be ashamed of enjoying poetry which older people tell you is sentimental or second-rate. The great thing is to enjoy *some* poetry: you will then be interested enough to go on and read more; and the more you read, the more you will develop a sort of instinct for telling the difference between first-rate and second-rate, between deep feeling and shallow sentiment.

You can also start very young to criticize the technique of poems. Epithets are perhaps the easiest things to begin with. Look at the epithets in poem B on pages 125–6: 'Little,' 'childish,' 'flower-strewn,' 'sweet.' As used in that poem, they're not very vivid or exciting, are they? They don't really add much to the force of the nouns they qualify: *'childish* feet,' *'sweet* heap of roses'—well of course roses are sweet, of course a child's feet are childish. These epithets aren't pulling their weight; they're just filling up gaps in the metre. How different from *'streaming* London's *central* roar,' where the epithets really make the picture, filling our ears and eyes with the noisy movement of traffic. It is the same with similes, metaphors, and the word-pictures we call images. When D. H. Lawrence writes of the bat flying at evening,

    A twitch, a twitter, an elastic shudder in flight

And serrated wings against the sky,
Like a glove, a black glove thrown up at the light
And falling back . . .

we feel we have seen the creature with our own eyes
—or rather, with eyes and imagination far sharper than our own. Remember, too, in criticizing the metaphors or images of a poem, it is not enough that they should be brilliant and exciting in themselves; they must also pull their weight by contributing something to the poem's theme, to its meaning as a whole.

Then there is the sound of a poem. You remember the second stanza of that passage from 'In Memoriam'?—

> Unloved, the sunflower, shining fair,
> Ray round with flames her disk of seed,
> And many a rose-carnation feed
> With summer spice the humming air.

Say it aloud. It's like eating a spicy plum cake. How does Tennyson get this extraordinary richness of sound into it? Chiefly by the repetition of certain vowel sounds—the úh sound in unl*o*ved, s*u*nflower, s*u*mmer, h*u*mming, and the broad ā of r*a*y, fl*a*mes, carn*a*tion, together with certain consonants, particularly the d's in unlove*d*, roun*d*, *d*isk, see*d*, fee*d*, and the m's in fla*m*es, *m*any, su*mm*er, hu*mm*ing. And all

WHEN IS A POEM NOT A POEM?

this rich fruitiness of sound is there for a purpose—to increase our sense of the richness and profusion of the summer flowers he is describing.

Again, you can criticize a poem's metre and rhythms. Discover first what the basic metre is— how many beats there are in each line: then, reading it aloud, notice what variations the poet has made on this basic metre; how he has quickened the pace of a line here, or slowed it down there; and ask yourself *why* he has done it. Is the rhythm varied, or monotonous? Does the poem run smoothly? Too smoothly? Heavily? Jerkily? Do some of the combinations of consonant sounds tie your tongue into knots? Does the end of a line too often coincide with the end of a phrase, or has the poet achieved variety by frequently running the sentences over from one line and ending them in the middle of the next one? Just as a good mechanic can tell, from the sound and rhythm of an engine, whether it is running properly, so can you with the sound and rhythm of a poem. And if it doesn't run sweetly, you can train yourself to look into its workings and find out what's wrong.

X

HOW TO ENJOY IT

Nearly all poetry gains from being read aloud. Rhythm, rhyme and repetition are conveyed more easily through the ear than through the eye; and therefore both the reader-aloud and the listener have an advantage over the person who is only reading a poem, with his eyes, to himself. The art of verse-speaking is a difficult one. A good voice is not enough in itself, any more than it is for a singer: the voice must be trained to express fine shades of meaning, to interpret—by changes of pace and tone and volume—the heart of the poem. But, if you have a genuine feeling for poetry, you can go some way towards teaching yourself how to speak it. Here are some hints on what to do and what not to do when you are speaking poetry.

1. Choose a poem which interests you and moves you. Sympathy between yourself and the poem is essential.

2. Don't try to make the poem sound dramatic unless it is a dramatic poem. Remember, you are a sort of musical instrument on which the poem is being played. So let the poem speak *through* you, and don't

HOW TO ENJOY IT

use it just as an opportunity for showing off your beautiful voice!

3. With lyric and contemplative poems, avoid like the plague any over-emphasis. Particularly, avoid emphasizing words just for the sake of variety, or because there happens to be a metrical stress on them. But avoiding over-emphasis and dramatization does not mean making the poem colourless. The chief way of bringing out the colour in a poem is to follow very carefully its rhythms and its changes of mood.

4. Follow the rhythms, and let the metre look after itself. For instance, the metre of these lines is—

> To trável líke a bírd, lightlý to víew
> Desérts where stóne gods fóunder ín the sánd. . . .

But if you read it like that, it will make ugly nonsense. How would you say it in the ordinary rhythm of speech?—

> To trável líke a bírd, líghtly to víew
> Désert where stóne góds foúnder in the sánd. . . .

Read it thus, and at once you get rid of the mechanical te-túmpty-túmpty-túmpty-túm which makes a poem sound like a wheezing old barrel-organ. I know that the quickest way to *learn* a poem is to use the tumpty-tum method; but, if you *speak it* that way, you deserve to have rotten eggs thrown at you.

5. Monotony and colourlessness are also avoided by *attack*. 'Attack' means speaking the words crisply and decisively, particularly the initial consonants of words. If you don't hit the beginning of a word hard, it won't be properly audible. For the same reason, don't let your voice fade away at the ends of words and phrases, and don't let it drop at the end of every line or sentence.

6. Make a slight pause at the end of every line; even if there is no stop there. The object of this is to tell the listener, who hasn't the written words in front of him, that the end of a line has been reached and thus convey to him the *form* of the poem. The sense may run straight on into the next line: but, unless you make this slight pause (it can often be done simply by lengthening the vowel-sound of the last syllable in the line), the poem's pattern becomes confused to the ear.

7. Tone and tempo. The tones of your voice should reflect the changing moods of a poem. But they will only do so if you yourself are sensitive to the poem—if you have felt its mysteriousness, its joy and its sadness. The tempo, or speed, at which you speak each line of a poem depends partly upon its rhythms, partly on its sense. In a ballad or dramatic poem, you can change speed more often and more abruptly than

in a lyric or contemplative one. But, when in doubt, let the rhythm be your guide.

8. Above all, speak simply and naturally. Don't put on an artificial voice: and don't speak the poem in a soulful monotone—unless you want to sound like a sick cow. But try to make your voice more flexible, using high notes and low, just as you do when talking to friends.

Choral Speaking

Verse-speaking in chorus, or 'choral speaking' as it is called, is one of the very best ways to enjoy poetry. It is as exciting as singing in a choir or playing in an orchestra; and it is grand to listen to. I have judged choirs at verse-speaking competitions—some of them came from schools—which made me feel the music of certain poems more keenly than I had ever felt it before. By 'music' here, I mean not only the musical sound of the words, but the rhythm and balance of the lines, and the way the ideas in the poem are developed like themes in music. Choral speaking has one obvious advantage over solo speaking: it offers greater variety. You can 'set' a poem for choral speaking so that some passages are spoken by the whole choir, others by a few voices or a single voice: and, in doing so, you bring out more clearly the meaning of the poem as a whole.

Turn back to the poem printed on pages 124–125 (ballads or narrative poems, like this one, offer the best opportunity for dramatic choral speaking, though choirs can give beautiful renderings of lyric and contemplative verse provided they do not play too many tricks with it). You will decide, perhaps, that the opening three lines of the poem should be spoken by three voices all together, the forth line by a single voice, and the last four lines (the refrain) by the whole choir. You may keep this pattern throughout the first three stanzas; or you may alter it, say, by having each line of the refrain spoken by a separate voice in stanza three, the voices echoing each other. No doubt you would use full choir to bring the poem to a strong climax in lines one to three of the last stanza, returning perhaps to a single voice for the last line of all. There's no better way of getting to understand the pattern of a poem than trying to arrange it for choral speaking.

I am not attempting to tell you how to train a verse-speaking choir, for this is a difficult, highly specialized job, which should only be undertaken by some one who has himself gone through the training.

A word in your ear

Boys and girls often ask me (particularly when their teachers are present) if I don't think it a bad thing for

HOW TO ENJOY IT

them to be compelled to learn poetry by heart in school. The answer is—Yes, and No. If you've got into the way of thinking that poetry is stupid stuff, or useless, or beneath your dignity, then you certainly won't get much out of learning it by heart. But remember that it is a good thing to train your memory, and learning a poem is at least a much pleasanter way of training it than learning, say, twenty lines out of the telephone directory. What is more important, to learn poetry is to learn a respect for words; and without this respect for words, you will never be able to think clearly or express yourself properly: and until you can do that, you'll never fully grow up—not though you live to be a hundred. A third good reason for learning poetry by heart is that, by doing so, you are sowing a harvest in yourself. It may seem to you at the time a dull, laborious business, with nothing to show for it: but, as you get a bit older, you'll find passages of poetry you learnt at school, and thought you had forgotten, thrusting up out of your memory, making life happier and more interesting.

Many of you, however, don't need any persuasion to learn poetry and aren't in the least ashamed of liking it (to be ashamed of liking poetry is just as absurd as to be ashamed of liking ice-creams: and to be proud of *not* liking it—well, you might as well be proud of not knowing how to ride a bicycle). For the lucky ones

who do like it, there are plenty of good poetry books in
which they can find every kind of poem by every kind
of poet. The best book of all, for your age, is—I
think—Walter de la Mare's 'Come Hither.' But no
printed book is quite as good as the one you make up
for yourself. So get some one to give you a smart-
looking manuscript book, and copy into it poems or
lines of poetry that take your fancy: if you can draw,
you'll make your book even nicer by doing coloured
decorations for each poem, or pictures illustrating the
themes of the poems.

Perhaps you'll write some poems yourself to put
into your book. Nobody can teach you to write poetry: but here are one or two hints you may find useful.
Use simple metres and short lines—the ballad metre
is a good one to start with—and don't worry too much
about the rhymes: rhymes are difficult to handle at
first, and the need for finding a rhyme is apt to prevent
you from saying what you want to say: better a bad
rhyme, or no rhyme, than a word which rhymes perfectly but makes the line sound silly. Secondly, don't
be afraid of using words—new words, old words,
curious words, long words, ordinary words, words
whose meaning you don't quite understand, words that
seem to be 'unpoetical': always be looking for more
words to use: every poem should be an experiment
in words; and every poem should flaunt words as

HOW TO ENJOY IT

proudly as a peacock flaunts its tail. Thirdly, write about things because they interest and touch you, not because they seem to you typical subjects for poetry. A street accident, a pet rabbit, a Spitfire, a good dinner, a visit to the seaside or the dentist—whatever shocks, pleases, frightens or excites you is material for poetry.

Describe it in rhythmical words, compare it with other things that thrill you, try to say what you yourself *feel* about it—and you'll be on the way to writing a poem.

* * * *

Now my book is finished. I have called it 'Poetry for You,' since this is what I've tried to do—to show you that poetry is something meant for *you* to enjoy, not a weird form of activity appealing only to grown-ups or eccentrics. I expect there may be things in the book which have puzzled you, or which you don't agree with. If your parents or teachers can't explain them, write to me (c/o the publisher) and ask me about them. This book is for you, and I want it to be as good as possible: so, if I get some interesting questions from my readers, I'll ask my publisher to let me write an extra chapter, answering them, to be included in the next edition of the book.

NOTES

I

WHAT IS THE USE OF POETRY?

Page Line
3. 3-4 **William Blake** (1757-1827) 英国の詩人にして画家. ロンドンの靴下職人の子に生れ, 学校には行かず, 彫版師の徒弟となり, 自からの詩集に彩飾を施した. 散文と理性の時代にあってロマン的, 神秘的な作品を書いた. 主なる作品は *Songs of Innocence, Songs of Experience* その他予言的, 諷刺的, 反逆的な詩が多数ある.

4 **William Cowper** (1731-1800) 同じくロマン主義の魁をなす詩人. *Task* 六巻に (1785) よって記憶されている. 自然を愛し, 都会をさけて田園に生活することをすすめた.

John Clare (1793-1864) 自然詩人. 英国ロマン主義の最盛期における二流詩人. (*cf.* p. 92)

4-5 **Christopher Smart** (1722-71) "Song to David" (1763) で有名な, ケンブリッジ大学出の詩人.——以上の四人は生涯の一部またはその終りを狂気の中に過したのであった.

4. 5-6 **Sir Philip Sidney** (1554-86) 最盛期にある Renaissance 時代の英国の華で, ここに述べられた男らしい最後に終った三十三年の短かい一生の間に, 政治に, 文学に, 植民事業に, 多彩な仕事を残した. 小説 *Arcadia*, ソネット集 *Astrophel and Stella* の他に英国詩論の源流をなす *Apologie for Poetrie* を書いた.

6. 17-8 "**My heart leaps up . . .**" Wordsworth の虹の歌の冒頭の二行. わが国でも人口に膾炙してるが念のため全行を引用する.

> My heart leaps up when I behold
>   A rainbow in the sky:
> So was it when my life began,
> So is it now I am a man,
> So be it when I shall grow old,
>   Or let me die!
> The Child is father of the Man,
> And I could wish my days to be
> Bound each to each by natural piety.

作者 William Wordsworth (1770-1850) は英国最大の自然詩人で, 後出の Coleridge と共に, 1798年詩集 *Lyrical Ballads*(「抒情歌謡集」)を発表して, 華やかな英国ロマン主義の幕を切って落した. 自然に対して一種神秘的な親和感をもち, 上掲の虹の歌の外, "The Daffodils," "To the Cuckoo," "Tintern Abbey Lines," "Ode on Intimations of Immortality" 等がよく知られている. その大作 "The Prelude" については pp. 94-96 参照.

7. 22 **"Bright is the ring of words"** R. L. Stevenson (1850-1894) の Songs of Travel 第十四の冒頭の一行. 次行は when the right man rings them とある. 真の詩人の手になるとき言葉は美しい響きを放つの意.

8. 15 **Tennyson,** Alfred (1809-1892) ヴィクトリア朝の代表詩人. 親友 Hallam の死を悼んだ挽歌 "In Memoriam" が彼の最初の傑作で, これを発表した 1850 年に Wordsworth の死の後を襲って桂冠詩人 (poet laureate) となり Browning と並んで一世を風靡した. 桂冠詩人とは古くから今日に至るまで英国に行なわれている制度で, 概ねその時代の代表的詩人が, 形ばかりながら王室の扶持を受けて, 国家的な出来事に際して詩を書く役目に選ばれるのである. Tennyson の詩は, 思想的に見て多少甘すぎるきらいはあるが, 最もよくその時代を代弁して居り, その巧みな詩語の駆使は, 甘美なメロディーによって多くの人々に愛誦された. "The wrinkled sea ..." の句は断片 "The Eagle" の第四行.

11. 26 **"I wandered lonely as a cloud ..."** Wordsworth の "The Daffodils" の第一節. ここで簡単に, この詩の第二節を引用して, 英詩の形式について述べよう. 英詩は強勢アクセント (stress accent) のある音節 (syllable) と無い音節との結合によるリズムに基づいて書かれる. 強勢のある音節を ′ の符号で表わし, 強勢のない音節を ⌣ で表わすと, この詩の第二節のリズムは次の様になる.

⌣ ′ ⌣ ⌣ ′ ⌣ ′ ⌣ ′
Continuous as the stars that shine
 ′ ⌣ ′ ⌣ ′ ⌣ ′
 And twinkle on the milky way,
⌣ ′ ⌣ ⌣ ′ ⌣ ′ ⌣ ′
They stretched in never-ending line
⌣ ′ ⌣ ′ ⌣ ′ ⌣ ′
 Along the margin of a bay:
 ′ ⌣ ′ ⌣ ′ ⌣ ′
Ten thousand saw I at a glance
 ′ ⌣ ⌣ ′ ⌣ ′ ⌣ ′
Tossing their heads in sprightly dance.

多少の破格はあるがこの詩の基本的なリズムの形は第二, 三, 四行の如く弱強の順に一組をなす音節が四つから成る一行に存することが分る. この弱強 (⌣′) の一組を iambus (抑揚格) と称し, これが四つより成る行で書かれた詩を iambic tetrameter (抑揚四音歩格) と呼ぶ. 他の例については後に出て来る場合について述べよう.

次に脚韻 (rhyme) について言えば, ある二行の最後の強勢ある音節の母音が (それに子音が続く時は子音も) 同音であるか, 又はその音節の後に強勢のない音節がついている場合にはその音節の母音も子音も同音である場合, その二行は「韻をふんでいる」と称する. そして強勢ある音節の母音の直前の子音は同一であるよりは異っているのを本格とする. 上記の例では第一行, 第三行の shine [ʃain] と line [lain] 第二, 第四行の way [wei] と bay [bei] 第五, 第六行の glance [glɑːns] と dance [dɑːns] とは上述の法則に照らして完全な韻をふんでいると言える. もし to sea と to see [共に tə siː] のごとき語に終る二行があればこれは完全な韻をふむと言われず, またもし ending [éndiŋ] と mending [méndiŋ] の二語に終る二行があれば, これは完全な押韻と言えるが ending と mended とでは, 最後の強勢のある音節の母音は同音でも, それ以後の音節が同音でないから half-rhyme と呼ぶ. (cf. p. 37)

単音節の語が強勢をもつか否かの大体の目安は, 名詞, 形容詞, 動詞等は強勢を有し, その他の品詞は強勢をもたぬと理解してよい. 然し実際に詩を読む場合には, 自然に, 意味をとりつつ, 各語の本来のアクセントに従って読むべきであって, 初めから, 例えば上記の詩は iambic tetrameter であるときめてしまって, その型を詩の上に押しつけてはならない. さもないと第五行目の Ten thousand は [ten θáuzənd] と読まなくてはならなくなり, 折角の 一万 という誇張が a thousand [ə θáuzənd] 一千と同じ様な力しかもたなくなる. tossing [tɔ́siŋ] を型に合せて [tɔsíŋ] などと読むのは論外である. この詩が iambic tetrameter であるというのは, 自然によむ中におのずと表われて来るリズムの平均的な型, または norm からおして, この詩の標準的な型がそうであるというまでのことである. metre とは, この様に現実の詩の背後にあってその詩に基調を与える, 一つの理想的なリズムの型と言ってよかろう. 更に一つ注意をすべきことは, 以上の如き事柄は, 凡べて詩を声に出して読んだ場合の音について言われることであって, 決して書かれた字についてのことではないという点である. 本来詩は耳に訴えるべきもので目に訴えるべきものではない. そしてリズムと音の響きが主であり, 押韻は従である. 現に押韻のない詩は古来から存在し, 近代の詩

にはことにそれが多い.

　以上の外, stanza (詩節) について言えば, 本文中にあるこの詩の第一節とここに引用した第二節は, 共に iambic tetrameter で, 押韻の型 (rhyme scheme という) は第一第三, 第二第四, 第五第六の各行が押韻している形である. この様に普通四行以上が集まり, 同じ rhyme scheme をもつものを stanza という. 勿論 stanza の形を用いない詩はいくらもあるが抒情詩は多くこれを用いる. (*cf*. p. 36)

13. 20–21 "**flash upon that inward eye ...**" 　上記 "The Daffodils" の第3節4行.

II

HOW POETRY BEGAN

17. 20–21 "**the cruel, crawling, hungry foam**" 　*cf*. Kingsley; The Sands of Dee, 11. 20–1.

　The cruel, crawling foam,

　The cruel, hungry form,

19. 14 "*Tell me, where is Fancy bred?*" 　Shakespeare: The Merchant of Venice. III. ii. 63.

　16 **Homer** 　p. 69, l. 11 註参照.

21. 22 "**The Ballad of the Revenge**" 　普通の題名は The Revenge で副題に A Ballad of the Fleet とある. The Revenge とは船の名で, 海軍提督 Sir Richard Grenville (1541?–91) がこれに乗り, 只一隻で十五隻のスペインの軍艦と十五時間闘い, 彼が致命傷をうけた史実を Tennyson が歌っているのである.

24. 5–6 **Persephone, Pluto, Ceres** 　は皆有名なギリシアの神々である. 但し Ceres はローマ人が呼んだ名で, 元来のギリシア名は Demeter である. ローマ人はギリシアの神々を多くそのまま, 名前だけを変えて引きついだ. ギリシアの Zeus を Jupiter に, Aphrodite を Venus に変えたように, Persephone もローマに入ると Proserpina と呼ばれる. 因に Demeter 即ち Ceres は小麦の女神で, 今日の英語 cereal はこの神の名に由来する.

25. 3 **Buonaparte**＝Bonaparte.

　6 **Beelzebub** 　は Bible に出て来る悪魔の名. Milton の "Paradise Lost" では Satan に次ぐ大悪魔とされている.

III

THE INSTRUMENTS OF POETRY

26. 13 "**Shall I compare thee ...**" Shakespeare の Sonnet XVIII の最初の二行. なおソネットとはイタリアから来た短詩で十四行からなり, そのリズムの型は ‿╱‿╱‿╱‿╱‿╱ 即ち iambus が五つで一行をなす. これを iambic pentameter と言う. 勿論一篇ごとに独立した詩であるが, しばしばある一つのテーマを中心にした連作の形をとる. これを sonnet sequence と称する. Shakespeare は百五十四篇の sonnet を書き, これが二つの sequence をなしている. この十八番の一篇はことに有名なものの一つである. " thee " と呼ばれている人物は, 作者の年下の美貌の青年貴族で, これが果して何人であるかについては色々の説があって明らかでない. その人物に対する詩人の想いを歌ったのが一番から百二十六番迄の Sonnet で, 残りの二十八篇はこれも神秘のとばりに閉ざされている "Dark Lady" を中心としている.

14 **temperate**＝of a mild temperature (Schmidt).

16 "**My love is like a red, red rose**" 作者 Robert Burns (1759-96) はスコットランドの詩人で, 貧しい農家に生れ, 苦しい労働と激しい恋の中に短い一生を終った. 日常卑近な事物や, 恋人に対する感情を, 卒直, 真摯に歌ったものが彼の詩で, スコットランド方言の駆使は, 強い郷土色をにじみ出させている. わが国の「螢の光」の歌は, 彼の有名な詩 " Auld Lang Syne " [ɔːld læŋ sain] (往にし昔の意) の曲に東洋流の歌詞をおきかえたものである. Burns の抒情詩はよく歌曲にされているが, それらの中では " My Heart's in the Highlands " はことに美しい.

27. 18 "**The winds that will be howling ...**" Wordsworth の " The World is too much with us; late and soon " に始まる sonnet の第六行. will＝refuse to be prevailed on not to (*C.O.D.*) *cf.* accidents will happen.

19 **up-gathered** 至る所を吹き廻る風が, どこかに集め収められて静まっている様を言う.

22 "**... yet still the sails made on ...**" S. T. Coleridge の傑作 " The Rime of the Ancient Mariner " Part 5, Stanza 18. 作者 Coleridge (1772-1834) は前述の Wordsworth と共に *Lyrical Ballads* を出版して英国ロマン主義の火蓋を切ったが, 後には主として

批評に向い，ドイツ哲学に基礎をおいた文芸批評により今日においても重きをなしている．詩としては上記の「老水夫の歌」の一篇，批評としては " Biographia Literaria " (「文学的自叙伝」) が主要作である．

28．3 " More beautiful and soft..." Stephen Spender [stíːvn spéndə] の " The Landscape near an Aerodrome " の始めの四行．作者は 1909 年生れの英国詩人で，英文壇における中堅どころの大家である．この詩に旅客用定期飛行機が描かれているように，機関車とか，鉄塔とか，在来の詩には扱われなかった近代科学文明の産物をよく歌っている．

29．7 Wotton, Sir Henry (1568-1639)　英国のヴェニス駐在大使となった外交官にして詩人．引用された詩行は，彼の最も有名な詩 " On his Mistress, the Queen of Bohemia " の第四行と五行．但し五行目の moon は sun が正しい．著者の記憶の誤りであろう．

15　**Vaughan** [vɔːn], Henry (1622-95)　いわゆる「形而上詩人」(Metaphysical poets) の一人で，宗教詩の優れたものを書いた．一種の神秘思想家 (mystic) である．引用された句は " Ascension-Hymn " (キリスト昇天の讃歌) の第十七行にある．

30．12 " Tyger! Tyger! burning bright..." は前出 Blake の " Songs of Experience " 中にある最も有名な詩の第一節．この詩のリズムは ′ ‿ ′ ‿ ′ ‿ でもしこの行末に一つの弱音節が省略されたものと見てよいならばこの詩は ′ ‿ 即ち trochee が四つある trochaic tetrameter であると云える．

19　**" Those green-robed senators..."** Keats の " Hyperion ", Book 1. ll. 73-4. 作者 John Keats (1795-1821) は典型的な英国ロマン主義詩人，僅か二十五年の生涯の中にあれ程の傑作をのこした彼の詩的才能は，まさに Shakespeare に匹敵するものである．上記 " Hyperion " は未完の作であり，長詩 " Endymion " は難解であるが，" La Belle Dame sans Merci " (「つれなきたをやめ」) " To Autumn " (「秋に寄す」) の如き小品は，英詩初学者の必読の傑作である．

31．2 Gerard Manley Hopkins (1844-89)　英国のカトリック詩人．ダブリン大学のギリシア語の教授．その詩は，彼の死後はじめて友人 Bridges によって出版された．独創的な詩人で現代英詩壇に大きな影響をあたえたがその作は難解である．" The Wreck of the Deutschland ", " The Windhover " が代表作．引用された一行は " Inversnaid " 第十二行．

32．19 " The bells that chimed..." " The Innocent " という詩の第二節．

NOTES

33. 4 **Malvern** [mɔ́:lvən *or* mɔ́:vən] **Priory** は Shakespeare の生地 Stratford on Avon で有名な Warwickshire の西隣りの Worcestershire [wústəʃiə] にある古い僧院。十四世紀の詩人 Langland はこの僧院で学んだろうと言われている。

18 **Thomas Nashe** [næʃ] (1567-1601) 小説家, 劇作家, また当時流行のパンフレットによる論争に加わった。引用された詩は "In Time of Pestilence" の第三節で, この四行の前に,

    Beauty is but a flower
    Which wrinkles will devour:

の二行が加わって一節をなす。pestilence と云われるのは, 今日のペストのみならず, 種々の激しい伝染病をも含めて呼んだものであろうが, 中世以来ヨーロッパはしばしばこの大流行に見舞われた。Nashe の詩に歌われたペストの流行は1593年のもので, ロンドンの劇場が二月から年末迄閉鎖されたほどであった。Helen はギリシア第一の美女。トロイ戦争のもととなった佳人で絶世の美人の典型である。Queen of Troy と呼ぶことは多少誤解を招くからちょっとつけ加えておくが, Helen はギリシアのスパルタの王 Menelaus の后で, これをトロイ王 Priam の次子 Paris が奪ってトロイに逃げたことから, ギリシアとトロイの大戦争になる次第が Homer の "Iliad" に歌われているのである。

34. 26 "**O sunflower, weary of time**" Blake の "Songs of Experience" 中の小品。普通は "O" ではなく "Ah" となっている。weary of time は「時に倦む」の意。毎日毎日太陽のあとのみを追っているひまわりの花によって, キリストとマリアの昇天した光明の世界にあこがれる人間の魂を象徴した詩。

35. 8 "**The wilderness and the solitary place . . .**" 旧約聖書, イザヤ書, 三十五章一節。

16 "**To be or not to be . . .**" Shakespeare: "Hamlet" 三幕一場の有名な Hamlet の独白。

36. 18 "**The Assyrian came down**" Byron の "The Destruction of Sennacherib" の第一行。Sennacherib とは聖書に言うセナケリブで, アッシリアの王。ユダの王ヒゼキヤを攻め滅ぼそうとしたが, 却ってユダヤ人の神エホバの力によって一夜に十八万五千人の兵を殺され, 敗退した。(イザヤ書三十七章, 列王紀略下, 十九章参照) 作者 George Noel Gordon, Lord Byron (1788-1824) は英国ロマン派詩人の驍将。跛の身をもってギリシア独立軍を助けようとして, 病死した一生は, 多くの女性との恋愛と共に, それ自身ロマンティックなものと言えよう。代表作の叙事詩 "Childe Harold", 叙事詩的諷刺詩 "Don Juan" 等

の他に多くの抒情詩がある. この一行の韻律は ⌣⌣′ 即ち anapaest が四つからなるもので anapaestic tetrameter と呼ぶ.

37. 1 " Break, break, break ..." Tennyson の有名な無題の短詩の第一行.

23-4 **assonances** これは弘法も筆の誤りというべきものであろう. assonance とは普通は強勢のある音節で同一の母音をくりかえすことをいう. 例えば fate—take; penitent—reticence. l. 22 の 'lightly' と 'frightful' がこれに当る. 著者が assonance と呼んでいるのは consonance のことである. Beckson and Ganz: *A Reader's Guide to Literary Terms* によれば consonance とは, 1. The close repetition of identical consonant sounds before and after different vowels, such as " flip—flop," " feel—fill." 2. Some writers accepts as consonance, the repetition of consonant sounds at the ends of words only, as in " east—west," or " hid—bed." ll. 25-p. 38, l. 1 にあげられた二例の初めの方は (1) に, 後の方は (2) に当る.

38. 17 " I hear lake water lapping ..." Yeats [jeits] の最も人に知られている詩 " The Lake Isle of Innisfree " の第十行目. W. B. Yeats (1865-1939) はアイルランドに生れた十九世紀末のアイルランド文芸復興の中心人物であり, また今世紀前半の英詩壇の第一人者. 詩の他に劇, エッセイ等作品は多い. 初期の詩は, 上記の一篇を含む 1895 年の「詩集」(*Poems*) 及び *The Wind among the Reeds* (1899) が主なるもので, その詩風は象徴的である. 我が国には早く明治, 大正の頃から紹介されていたが, 本格的な研究はまだ行われていない.

21 **" Dry clashed his armour ..."** Tennyson のこの一行は著書の misquotation で armour ではなく harness が正しい. " Morte d'Arthur " (「アーサー王の死」) 百八十六行.

IV

HOW A POEM IS MADE

44. 13 " The mind in creation is as a fading coal ..." (Shelley) *Defence of Poetry* (研究社版 *English Critical Essays*, p. 68). Percy Bysshe Shelley (1792-1822) は Keats, Byron と共にロマン派詩人の花形. イタリアのスペチア湾で嵐のためヨットが難破して溺死した最後まで実にロマンティックである. " Prometheus Unbound " (「プロミーシュース解縛」), " Ode to the West Wind " (「西風の賦」) 等の傑作

NOTES 149

を残し,その理想主義的な革命的精神によって青年の心を惹きつけている.

21 "**Children look down upon...**" C. Day Lewis 自作のsonnet. ソネットが iambic pentameter の詩であることは前に述べたが,更にこの作品についてもう少し詳しく述べると,十四行が8行—6行の二つのグループに分れ前者を octave 後者を sestet と呼ぶ. octaveはまた 4-4 と二つの quatrain に分れる. 大体において漢詩の絶句のように起承転結という最も完全な芸術的形式にのっとっていると見ることが出来るもので,始めの quatrain 二つ,即ち octave で起承が sestet で転結が歌われる. 脚韻はこの詩では第一と第四,第二と第三,第五と第八,第六と第七が各々韻をふんでいる (不完全な韻もあるが). sestet は第九と第十二,第十と第十一,第十三と第十四が各々韻をふんでいるらしい. 詳しいことは省くが,これは本格的なイタリアの詩型に忠実な型の英国ソネットで Milton がその代表作者. Shakespeare のソネットは多少異り,三つの quatrain と一つの couplet 即ち二行の対句からなる. 脚韻のふみ方もまた違っている.

24 **roundabout**=merry-go-round. (*cf.* pp. 85-87)

V

POEMS THAT TELL A STORY

52. 8 **chimbley**=chimney.

   10 **anovver**=another.

53. 16 **ballad** *cf.* p. 63, l. 6 の註.

54. 23-4 **Admiral Benbow** は英国の提督で, 1702 年西インド諸島でフランス艦隊と戦い,両足を砕かれたがひるまず,木の框にすがって指揮をとったという.

57. 2 **wouldna**=would not.

58. 27 **the Icomb Mummers' Play** Mummers' Play については第二章の終りに,著者の解説があったが,これは古くから England, Scotland, Ireland, Wales の各地に行われ,St. George Play と呼ばれて地方により筋に異同がある. Icomb は地名か?

59. 1 **Old Hind-before** 何のことやら分らない.

   2 **fust** first の俗語か?

   14 **a crust of her ale** は次行の a glass of her bread and cheese とごちゃごちゃになったもの. つまり a glass of her ale と a crust

of her bread and cheese の首をすげ替えたもの.

16 **"Yes thanks", "No please"** も同じ手で, 普通なら "Yes please", "No thanks" であろう.

18 **Bacca-Carn** 意味不明. 元来は何か意味があったのが分らなくなったものだろう.

19 **t'other**=the other.

22 **hollow**=hello, to cry out loud, to shout.

60. 5 **ITMA** *It's that Man Again* という本の名らしい.

15 **Western Mail**=Western Pacific Line (Salt Lake—San Francisco 間の鉄道) の郵便列車.

17 **rounder**=an idle frequenter of public resorts.

19 **hogger**=the driver of locomotive (Partridge).

61. 4 **out**=out of (Americanism).

10 **'Frisco**=San Francisco. **but**=if not, unless.

17 **Number Four** 列車の番号か？

22 **roads**=rail-roads.

24 **S.P.**=South Pacific (Railway).

26 **pink**=an urgent telegram (Partridge).

28 **Salt Lake line** Western Pacific Line のこと.

62. 21 ***"A plume in his helmet..."*** 未詳.

63. 4 **With a link a down a day** 一種の refrain で別に意味はない. この詩の中には "with a link a down a down" という形も出ている. また "Robin Hood's Death and Burial" という ballad には "Down a down, a down, a down" という例もある.「よいやさ」「こらさ」の類. (*cf.* p. 54, l. 7. "Bow down! Bow down!)

5 **silly**「あわれな」

6 **Was weeping**=who was weeping. ballad は古い英国の民謡で現存している最古のものは十五世紀頃に生れたもの. 短かい stanza をつらねた簡単な詩で伝説や物語を力強く, 生き生きと描いているのが常である. 元来は, ダンスに合せて歌った歌から変ったものと言われる. Robin Hood を歌ったものや後に出ている "Chevy Chase" 等が代表的な ballad である. 最も普通な形は iambic tetrameter ($\smile/\smile/\smile/\smile/$) と iambic trimeter ($\smile/\smile/\smile/$) を交互において四行となし, 二行と四行目が韻をふむものである.

21 **"Sir Patrick Spens"** Robin Hood や "Chevy Chase" と並んで有名な ballad. Sir Patrick Spens がスコットランド王の娘をノールウェイに送り届け, その帰路, 嵐に難破して死ぬことを歌ったも

NOTES

の.

 22 **yestreen**=yesterday evening.
 23 **auld**=old.
 24 **gang**=go.

64. 1 **hadna**=had not.
 2 **A league but barely three**=barely three leagues.
 3 **lift**=sky (原註).
 4 **gurly**=wild (原註).

65. 8 "*Of moving accidents by flood and field*" Shakespeare: "Othello," I. iii. 135.

 12 "**Chevy Chase**" England の北辺 Northumberland の領主 Percy が狩猟のため Scotland に侵入し, その地の領主 Douglas と闘い, 終に二人共戦死する物語を歌った勇壮な ballad. Chevy (或いは Cheviot) は丘陵地の名. chase は狩猟の意.

66. 6 **hae ye**=have you.
 10 **wald**=would.
 11 **gat**=got.
 19 **broo**=broth (Scotch).

68. 9 "**The Ancient Mariner**" 既にその一部が引用されたが, この詩のあら筋はこうである. 一人の老水夫が結婚式によばれてゆく男を呼びとめて次のような自分の体験を語る——彼の乗船が嵐に会い南極の方に流されたときに, 信天翁 (albatross) を射殺した. この残忍な行為の酬いで彼の船に呪がふりかかり, 赤道まで吹き戻されてそのまま凪のために船が動かなくなった. 船員は, 飲料水の不足に苦しみ死にたえて, 終に彼一人となってしまう. だがこの呪も, 彼が海蛇の泳ぎ廻るのを見てその美しさに打たれ, 愛の心が醒めて海蛇を祝福したときに消え去って, 彼は無事に英国に帰ることが出来たが, 罪の償いとして, 絶えず地方を歩き廻り, 自分の行ないを例にひいて, 神に造られた凡ゆる生き物に対する愛と尊敬を人に教える運命を負わされる.

 卓絶した自然描写と無気味な, また神秘的な水夫の運命とを織り交ぜて, 作者の宗教観から見た人間の心と運命を描いて間然する所がない. Coleridge の最大傑作であるばかりでなく, ballad 形式による英詩の頂点に立つ作品である. 引用の節は Part 7. Stanza 23.

69. 11 "**Iliad**" と "**Odyssey**" とは Homer の手になる古典ギリシア叙事詩の最高峯である. 然し Homer なる詩人がいかなる人であったか, また彼が果してこの二篇の真の作者であったか否かについては確実な典拠はない. 伝説によると彼は, 紀元前九乃至十一世紀の盲目詩人

で，生地は Smyrna, Rhodus その他五カ所がその名誉を争っている．
"Iliad" は前にも触れたように，ギリシア第一の美女で，スパルタ王 Menelaus の后，Helen が Troy の王子 Paris に奪われたことに端を発したギリシアの諸王とトロイ王との十年間に亘る大戦争の物語りであるが，その中の主な出来事は，ギリシア方第一の英雄 Achilles がトロイ方から奪った捕虜の女の分配から総大将 Agamemnon と不和を生じ，陣中に引きこもってギリシア方の旗色が悪くなる．ギリシア方はやむを得ず Achilles の親友 Patrocles に Achilles の鎧をきせてトロイ方の総大将 Hector と一騎打をさせ，彼が Hector に殺されると，Achilles は奮然として Hector に戦を挑みこれをたおす．然し彼も又 Hector の弟，この戦の張本人たる Paris の毒矢を踵にうけて死ぬ——という有名な挿話である．

"Odyssey" は上述のトロイ戦争に従軍したギリシア方第一の智将で，トロイ落城は彼の考案した名高い木馬の奇計によるのであるが，戦終って故国 Ithaca に帰る途中幾多の難に会い (lotus-eaters の挿話，Cyclops の難，風神 Aeolus の風袋の話，Siren の危難，Circe の魔術，Calypso の誘惑等すべて有名な物語りである) 十二年の後にやっと帰国し，貞節を守り通した妻 Penelope をとりまく悪者共を，息子 Telemachus と共に退治する．Ulysses は Odysseus のラテン名．

"**Aeneid**" [íːnid] はローマ最大の詩人 Virgil [və́ːdʒil] (70-19 B.C.) の傑作．これまたトロイ戦争の後日譚の一つ．主人公 Aeneas [i(ː)níːæs or íːniæs] はトロイ王 Priam の女婿で，トロイ落城の火焔をくぐりぬけ廿隻の船に一族郎党をのせて海に逃げる．彼が最後に Tiber 河にたどりつき，ラテン人の王になるまでの七年間の放浪の旅がこの叙事詩の内容をなしている．カルタゴの近くに難破して，女王 Dido と恋におちるが，神の命によって彼は去り，Dido が自殺する物語はその中でも有名である．なお著者 Lewis は最近 "Aeneid" の英訳を完成した．

12 "**Paradise Lost**" は英国叙事詩の最大傑作．作者 John Milton (1608-74) は Shakespeare につぐ詩人で，Cambridge 大学を出ラテン語に造詣が深かったために Cromwell のラテン語秘書をつとめたが，彼の死後，失意の上に既に盲目となっており，財産は没収され，結婚生活はうまくゆかず，一時やめていた作詩の中に引籠ることを余儀なくされた．"Paradise Lost"「失楽園」はこのような事情のもとにあった詩人が渾身の力をこめて書き上げた大叙事詩で，一万行にあまる長篇である．最初のスケッチから刊行まで(1667)には実に廿五年の歳月が費されている．十二巻より成り，その骨子は，神を凌がんとして謀叛を起

し，失敗して奈落におとされたかつての大天使 Lucifer 即ち Satan は部下を集めて再び神に挑み，最近神が創造して愛している人間を堕落させることによって復讐をとげようとして，終に Eden の園に蛇と化して Eve をそそのかし，Adam と Eve に神の禁じた智慧の木の実を食べさせる．この罪により二人は楽園を追われるが，大天使 Michael [máikl] は人間の子孫に起ること——救世主の出現，その死と復活と昇天，教会の堕落と救世主の再臨——を二人に語る．

詩形は iambic pentameter で韻をふまぬもの．即ち blank verse である．

12-3 **"Paradise Regained"** は前者の続篇．四巻から成り，専ら荒野に於けるキリストに対する Satan の誘惑を描いたもの．Adam と Eve が Satan の誘惑に負けて失った楽園が，キリストが同じ Satan の誘惑に打勝つことによって取戻される．詩的価値は "Paradise Lost" には及ばない．

14 **Chaucer,** Geoffrey (1340?-1400) 英詩の父と言われる大詩人．フランス，イタリアの文学，またその両者を通じてラテン文学を英国に輸入し，英文学の基を開いた．その最大傑作が "The Canterbury Tales" である．これは，春陽四月（旧暦）の候となると，毎年ロンドンから大本山 Canterbury の教会に参詣する巡礼の一行が，旅の長さを忘れるために各々物語りを述べる，という結構をもった一万七千行に及ぶ長詩で，その序詩につづく物語の語り手には騎士あり，粉屋あり，家扶，商人，市井の女房，司祭に尼僧院長，托鉢僧に法学生，料理人に免罪符売り等々，当時の社会のあらゆる階級の人々を網羅して，その語る物語は実に中世英国の一大絵巻の観がある．

25 **Masefield,** John (1878-1967) 前代の英国桂冠詩人．若い頃船乗りとなり，アメリカで苦しい下積みの生活を送った．この体験が後に彼の海洋詩や叙事詩に結晶したのである．彼が文壇に登場したのが "Salt Water Ballads" (1902) で Day Lewis がここにあげている I. 46 と 52 の二篇は "Port of Many Ships" と "Mother Carey" であるが，より人々に膾炙している詩としては "Sea-Fevre" と "Cargoes" の二篇がある．物語詩としては "The Everlasting Mercy", "The Daffodil Fields", "Dauber" その他がある．詩の他に小説もあり，多作の人であるが，今日の文壇ではもはや過去の人である．

70. 8 Robert Browning (1812-89) Tennyson と双壁をなすヴィクトリア朝中期の代表的詩人．*Men and Women, Dramatis Personae* 等の詩集，長篇物語詩 "The Ring and the Book" 等が主要な作品である．彼の最も得意とした手法は dramatic monologue （劇的独白）で

あって，これは恰も電話で話す二人の人物の対話の一方のみを書き読者をして蔭の声を想像せしめることによって，語り手の心理，性格，物語等を立体的に盛り上げるやりかたで，ここにあげられている "My Last Duchess," はその一例である．文芸復興期のあるイタリアの侯爵が，客に自分の死んだ先妻の肖像画を見せながら語る独白によって，読者は公爵が妻を殺害したらしい事実と，女の愛情などは全く分らない彼の冷たい打算的な，陰険な心を知るのである． "The Pied Piper of Hamelin" は子供におなじみのドイツの伝説，Hamelin を鼠の害から救った笛吹きの物語である．

21 **"Marmion"** 十六世紀の英国を舞台とした Scott の叙事詩． Henry VIII の寵臣 Lord Marmion が Sir Ralph de Wilton の婚約者 Lady Clare に横恋慕して悪だくみによって男を殺し Clare と結婚しようとするが，波瀾に富んだ一連の出来事の末，終に Marmion は Folden におけるスコットランド軍との戦で戦死し，de Wilton と Clare は結ばれるという筋である．引用されている詩行は，この合戦におけるスコットランド軍の善戦を描いたもの．作者 Sir Walter Scott (1771–1832) はスコットランド生れの小説家，詩人で，Wordsworth, Coleridge と共にロマン主義復興に与って力があった．小説は歴史小説で，三十数篇あり，我国でも，古くから有名な "Ivanhoe" はもとより，"Kenilworth", "Rob Roy" 等今日も読まれる名作である．詩としては上記の "Marmion" の他に "The Lady of the Lake" がよく知られている．

23 **make good** 「維持する」

24 **Their dark impenetrable wood** 王をとり囲んで守るスコットランド槍兵の槍の林．

71. 1 **Lord Macaulay,** Thobias Babington (1800-59) 政治家，文人，明治時代の我国によく読まれた人で，「英国史」「随筆集」及びここにあげられた "Lays of Ancient Rome" (「古代ローマ譚詩集」) が主なる作品である．後者はローマの歴史の源となったが，今は散逸してしまったローマの古歌謡を英語で再現しようとした試みであって，Horatius Cocles の物語の他に "Virginia", "The Battle of Lake Regillus", "The Prophecy of Capys" 等を含む．

6 **Jean Ingelow** [ín(d)ʒilou] (1820-97) 女流詩人．子供のための物語を書いた．最も有名な詩がこの高潮の詩である．

NOTES

VI

MOODS, VISIONS AND SEASONS

74. 16 **"Come unto these yellow sands"** Shakespeare: Tempest, I. 2. **"Where the bee sucks"** Tempest, V. 1. **"Full fathom five"** Tempest, I. 2. **"Blow, blow, thou winter wind"** As You Like It, II. 7. **"Come away, Death"** Twelfth Night, II. 4. **"Take, oh take those lips away"** Measure for Measure, IV. 1. **"Fear no more the heat o' the sun"** Cymbeline, IV. 2. この歌は, 疲労を恢復する薬だと思って飲んだ麻薬のために仮死状態に陥った Imogen (故あって男装している) を実の妹とは知らぬながらも, ふとした廻り合わせから, 一諸に住む様になり, 深い愛着を感じていた二人の兄, Guiderius と Arviragus とが, てっきり死んだものと思いこんで悲しみ歌う挽歌である.

75. 1 **Golden** = wealthy, high-born (Deighton).

4 **stroke** = the agency of any hostile and pernicious power (Schmidt).

7 **physic** = the art of healing diseases ('').

10 **thunder-stone** = thunderbolt ('').

14 **Consign to** = come to the same state, submit to the same terms ('').

15 **No exorciser harm thee** = May no exorciser disturb your spirit by calling it up from the grave in which we have laid you to rest! (Deighton).

17 **Ghost unlaid** 成仏しきれずに此の世に迷い出て来る亡者.

19 **Quiet consummation have** = May you enjoy a peaceful close to your life's trouble (Deighton). consummation は成仏の意.

76. 11 **Dekker,** Thomas (1570?-1632) Shakespeare と同時代の劇作家. 当時の多くの劇作家と合作をした. 代表作は "The Honest Whore", "The Shoemaker's Holiday" 等. "Lullaby" [lʌləbai] は "Patient Grissil", IV. ii.

Campion, Thomas (d. 1619) Dekker と同じくエリザベス朝の抒情詩人. "A Lamentation" も美しい詩であるが, "There is a garden in her face" の行に始まる "Cherry-Ripe" が最も有名な詩である.

12 **Ben Jonson** (1572-1637) Shakespeare に対立して，一大勢力をもっていたエリザベス朝の劇作家．"Every Man in his Humour"(「十人十色」) という劇で名声を博した．いわゆる comedy of humour (気質喜劇) の大家で，人間が各自の気質の故におかす失敗や愚かさを冷酷に描き，写実的に当時の市民生活を諷刺した．また "Sejamus" の如き悲劇，宮廷のための Mask (仮面劇) も書いている．

"**Slow, slow, fresh fount**" は "Cynthia's Revels"(「月の饗宴」) というエリザベス女王，今日ではエリザベス一世の宮廷を舞台とした軽い喜劇の中にある歌．Cynthia はギリシァの月の女神 Artemis (ローマ名 Diana) の別名で，エリザベス女王をこれに擬することは当時の詩人の常套手段であった．

13 **Peel,** George (1558?-97?) Peele とも書く．俳優兼劇作家．抒情詩をよくした．"The Arrainment of Paris" "The Old Wives' Tale" 等の劇がある．"His golden locks" は *Polyphymnia* (1950) と云う詩集の中にある．Thackeray の *The Newcomes* に引用されて有名になった．

78. 3-4 "**simple, sensuous, passionate**" Milton の論文 "Tractate of Education" の中にある言葉．詩の定義として有名である．

12-3 "**Have you seen but a bright lily grow**" Ben Jonson の "A Celebration of Charis" という詩からの引用．Charis は女性の名前で "The Triumph of Charis" という詩もある．第一行は Day Lewis の *The Echoing Green* では bright lily が white lily となっている．何れが正しいか未だ確かめ得ない．

13 **but** 二行下の but と共にリズムの上から入れられたもので，意味はないもの，つまり無用の文字であろう．このような例は O.E.D. にも見当らない．

20 **smelt o' the bud** o' は of で smell が自動詞に用いられている．今日の英語なら smell at の方が普通である．

21 **i'**=in.

80. 8 **were forsworn** は受身の形で "to be guilty of perjury" すなわち「偽証の罪ある」「嘘を言った」の意味をもつ．

81. 7 "**The Schoolboy**" と "**The Echoing Green**" はここに云われているように共に Blake の詩で，後者は著者 Day Lewis が本書と並行して読まれるように編纂した，子供の為の詩集の題に選ばれている．

18 "**O rose thou art sick**" "Tyger! Tyger!" の詩と共に "Songs of Experience" の中の最も有名な小品である．

82. 1 **"The silver swan..."** 白鳥は普段は鳴かぬが，死ぬ前にだけ鳴くと言われている．それで辞世の歌を swan song と呼ぶのである．ついでながら swan は英語ではスウォンである．アメリカ人はスワンと言うかも知れないが．

83. 16 **Thomas Hardy** (1840–1928) 小説家．詩人．我国に最もよく知られた小説家であるが，詩の方は一般には殆ど知られていない．*Tess of the D'Urbervilles*, *Jude the Obscure* 等多くの有名な小説があるが，彼の最大作といわれる *The Dynasts* は叙事詩劇 (epic-drama) である．詩人としてもまた一家をなしていると言うべきであろう．引用された "This is the weather the cuckoo likes" (題名 "Weathers") も愛すべき小品である．

21 **betumble** は betumbled (tossed in confusion, disordered) という Shakespeare 時代の過去分詞から作った動詞で Shakespeare にもこの形は見当らない．(栗の花穂を) 乱す．

24 ***The Traveller's Rest*** は inn 即ち旅館兼居酒屋の名であろう．

84. 12 **"O blithe New-comer!..."** の詩は Wordsworth の最も有名な詩 "The Cuckoo" である．

85. 10 **still**＝always.

86. 23 **"That time of year..."** Shakespeare: Sonnet LXXIII.

25 **"When I consider..."** Milton の Sonnet の中でも最大の傑作の一つ．中年にして視力を失った詩人の切々たる訴えで，題名は "On his Blindness"

26 **"The world is too much..."** 前出．以上の三篇はみな英国 sonnet の白眉である．

87. 15 **"Lycidas"** [lísidæs], **"Adonais"** [ædənéis], **"In Memoriam"** の三篇は英国の三大エレジーと云われるもの．"Lycidas" は Milton が友人 King の，"Adonais" は Shelley が Keats の，"In Memoriam" は Tennyson が親友 Hallam の死を悼んで作った詩である．

23 **Wilfrid Owen** (1893–1918) 第一次世界大戦に戦死した青年詩人．"Futility" は戦友の死を前にして神の意図を疑う心を歌った短詩である．原文には Wilfrid とあるが Wilfred が正しい．

88. 3 **Vaughan** 前出．"I see them walking..."の詩行は "Ascension-Hymn" の第三節にある．them は昇天した霊をさす．

12 **"Unwatch'd, the garden..."** "In Memoriam", CI.

14 **gather brown** 「紅葉の色を深める」

22 **the lesser wain**＝ursa minor すなわち小熊座．

90. 6 *"Ye Presences of Nature!"*　Wordsworth: "The Prelude" 中の言葉. (*cf.* p. 96, l. 22) Presences 諸霊. presence＝a divine, spiritual, or incorporeal being or influence felt or conceived as present (*O.E.D.*)

18　**"To see a world in a grain of sand..."**　Blake: "Auguries of Innocence" (「無染のうらかた」)「これらの箴言風の詩句に盛られている想像の活動が無染を察知する占象となる……」(寿岳文章「ブレイク抒情詩抄」註より)

91. 16 **Spenser,** Edmund (1552-99)　Chaucer の死後不振に陥った英国詩を再び大陸諸国の水準にまで高めエリザベス朝の最盛期の源を開いた詩人. "The Faerie Queene" は彼の傑作で, 未完ではあるが, 六巻余り, 三万三千行を越える大作である. 各巻が一つのテーマをもった allegory (寓意物語) で, 第一巻は神聖の徳を第二巻は中庸の徳を, そして第三巻では貞節の徳を物語によって描くといった風である. また彼の祝婚歌 "Prothalamion", "Epithalamion" は抒情詩の逸品. "Shepherd's Calendar" は牧歌の伝統を復活した画期的な試みであった.

"The Echoing Green" III. 114 に引用されているのは第七巻の二十八節から三十一節までで第三十節は次の如きものである.

>　　Then came the Autumne all in yellow clad,
>　　As though he ioyed in his plentious store,
>　　Laden with fruits that made him laugh, full glad
>　　That he had banisht hunger, which to-fore
>　　Had by the belly oft him pinched sore.
>　　Upon his head a wreath that was enrold
>　　With ears of corn, of euery sort he bore:
>　　And in his hand a sickle he did holde,
> To reape her ripened fruits the which the earth had yold.

綴りは古いままであるが大体想像がつくであろう. 発音も今日のそれとは多少異っていたが, 我々が味わう上に大した障碍はない. (l. 2 ioyed＝joyed; to-fore＝before; euery＝every; the which＝which; yold＝yielded.) 詩形はいわゆる Spenserian stanza と呼ばれるもので, ⏑ˊ⏑ˊ⏑ˊ⏑ˊ⏑ˊ すなわち iambic pentameter 八行と, さらにもう一つ十二音節の iambic hexameter (一名 Alexandrine) 一行とから成る九行の stanza で, 押韻は第一, 第三 (clad-glad), 第二, 第四, 第五, 第七 (store—to-fore—sore—bore) 第六, 第八, 第九 (enrold—holde—yold) となっている. 以上をひっくるめて言うと, 「iambic pentameter 八行と Alexandrine 一行の九行からなり, "a b a b b c b c c" の rhyme

scheme (押韻形式) をもつものを Spenserian stanza と呼ぶ.」となる.
Byron の "Childe Harold's Pilgrimage" はこの詩形を用いている.
92. 26 "The restless heat seems twittering by" 前出 John
Clare の "The Shepherd's Calendar" より.
93. 2 "And waddle in the water-pudge..." 同じく Clare の
"Little Trotty Wagtail" より. 第一行に四つの w を語頭に用いてあ
ることに注意. この様な技巧を alliteration (頭韻) という. **pudge**=
puddle.

6 **"While, far above..."** 上記 "The Shepherd's Calendar"
より.

9 **Crank**=to make a harsh, jarring, or grating sounds. (*O.E.D.*
citing this line)

20 **"The Prelude"** 十四巻から成る Wordsworth の自伝的な詩.
Coleridge に呼びかけたもので, 幼少の頃からの思い出を通じて, 彼の
汎神論的な自然観, 人生観が窺われる.

95. 13 Edmund Blunden (1896–1974) 我国に最も縁の深い詩人. 1924–
7 年東京大学で教え, また戦後英国文化使節として来朝し, 我々に深い
感銘を与えた. 日本に対する深い理解と同情とは, 温厚な人格, 深い学
識と相まって, 日英間の文化的なかけ橋の役割をつとめている. 多くの
田園詩の他に, 第一次大戦の従軍の体験を綴った散文 "Undertones of
War" (『戦争余韻』), John Clare, Christopher Smart の詩の編纂,
多くの英国文人の評論や伝記等の著作がある.

14 **hop-pole**=a tall pole on which hop-plants are trained (*O.E.D.*)
ホップの支柱.

96. 13–4 "in the midst of life we are in death" "The Book of
Common Prayer" (『英国教会祈禱書』) の中の句. 埋葬の時に墓前でと
なえるもの.

97. 10–1 "in the eye of the beholder" 古諺 "Beauty lies in the
eye of the beholder."

14 **Arnold,** Matthew (1822–88) 詩人. 批評家. 英国の近代的批評
の開祖とも言うべき人で, 批評家としては一流であるが, 詩人としては
一流とは言えぬであろう. 然し近代的な不安と幻滅を歌った詩人として
は A. H. Clough [klʌf] と共に英国で最初の人であった. この Clough
は Arnold の年長の友人で, その死を悼んだエレジーが "Thyrsis" で
ある. Arnold の傑作の一つで前記の "Lycidas", "Adonais", "In
Memoriam" と共に英国四大エレジーの一つと見る批評家もある. この
詩の美しさの半ばは, Oxford 近郊の山河の自然を歌った所にあり, こ

の点 Oxford の古い伝説に取題して心の悩みを歌った "Scholar Gipsy" と共に, Oxford とは縁の深い作品である. 散文としては "Culture and Anarchy", "Essays in Criticism" 二巻等が昔から我国においても広く読まれている.

VII

POETRY WITH A PURPOSE

99. 13 **Pope,** Alexander (1688–1744) 十八世紀前半を代表する詩人. いわゆる理神論的自然観, 理性の時代の代弁者で, Dryden の後をついで古典主義の文学観に立つその思想は, "Essay on Criticism" や "Essay on Man" 等の韻文による批評によっても知られるが, 決して平凡な理知一点張りの人ではなく, 強烈な創作慾と, 畸形の軀に宿った天才の激しい嫉妬, 羨望, 競争心を深く蔵しており, この点同様な運命の重荷をになった画家ロートレックや Byron を思わせる. 実際後者は, この点に共感する所あってか, Pope を非常に尊敬した. 卓絶した詩的技巧と鋭い理智, 辛辣な諷刺と皮肉を縦横に駆使した彼の satire はその種の詩の絶品であるが最も有名な作品は "Dunciad" (「固陋の徒」) で彼の仇とする当時の文人をなでぎりにしている. また彼の代表作としては "The Rape of the Lock" (「毛髪盗み」) と Homer の二大叙事詩の翻訳を忘れてはならない. ただし後者については, 英国における古今を通じて最大の古典学者の一人と言われる, 同時代人 Bentley は実に立派な出来であるが Homer ではないと評したという.

100. 25 **Marlowe,** Christopher (1564–93) Shakespeare と同年生れの劇作家. 文芸復興期の人間主義を端的に, 力強くうたった作品により, Ben Jonson をして "Marlowe's mighty line" の言葉を吐かせた. "Dr. Faustus" [fɔ́ːstəs] においては無限の知識に対する欲望を, "Tamburlaine the Great" では無限の権力に対する欲求を, また "The Jew of Malta" では無限の金銭欲, 物欲を描いている. 劇詩のための韻文として blank verse (無韻の iambic pentameter) を使用することにおいて Shakespeare の先駆をなし, 有望な劇作家であったが, 当時の政界の大立物 Walsingham [wɔ́ːlsiŋəm] のスパイの役を秘かに引受けていたのが原因となり, 酒屋での口論から刺殺されて短い一生を終った.

Webster, John (1580–1625?) エリザベス朝の劇作家. 多くの作家と喜劇を合作しているが, その悲劇 "The White Devil", "The

Duchess of Malfi" 等の名作においては，Shakespeare の壘に肉迫している．今世紀初頭の H. J. C. Grierson や T. S. Eliot による「形而上詩人」の再評価以来，彼の名もまた我国において広く知られるようになった．

101． 9 *"Teach me, my God and King"* 後出の George Herbert の詩 "The Elixer" の第一行．

18 **Nativity Plays** クリスマスに演ずる劇．特別のジャンルとしての名称ではない．

Miracle Plays 中世に生れ，十五，六世紀に最も栄えた宗教劇．教会の聖史や聖人達の伝説に基づいたもので，その最も古いものは "The Harrowing of Hell"（『地獄の掠奪』）で，キリストが地獄に下り，サタンの手から Adam その他の人々を奪いかえすという筋のものである．喜劇的要素を多く含みこの点が後代の劇に影響を及ぼしている．これはクリスマス以外の祭日にも行われた． passion play と呼ばれるものもこの一種で，キリストの受難を扱ったものをさす．

21 **Morality Plays** moralities とも呼ばれる．同じく中世の韻文劇で，Miracle Plays の登場者が聖書中の人物であるに反して，これでは vice とか virtue（悪玉善玉）の如き抽象的概念の擬人化されたものが出て来る．筋は単純で教訓を目的とした．十五世紀のものが多く，その代表的なものである "Everyman" は，人間一般を代表する Everyman なる人物が，死ぬ時になって，友も身内も，財産も知識も，美も，力も，自分について来てくれず，ただ善行のみが死出の旅路の同行となってくれたという筋である．言うまでもなく，財産とか知識とかはみな人物として登場する．

102． 1 **a-walking** 次行の a-sailing 同様今日なら a は不用である． a は away, on 等の意味であると言われるが，文法的，語学的説明は省略する．

7 **makeless**＝matchless（原註）．

9 **ches**＝chose（同前）．

22 **maiden** とは処女マリア．king of all kings はキリストをさす．

103． 10 **Achilles, Hector** p. 69, l. 11 の註参照．

13 **Andrew Marvell** (1621–78) Milton の後輩でその友人．「形而上詩人」の一人と見なされている．Day Lewis が "The Echoing Green" に載せているのは "Bermudas", "Thoughts in a Garden" の一部，"Mower, to Glow-worms" の三篇であるが，"To his Coy Mistress" が彼の抒情詩の最大傑作であり，また「形而上詩」の典型というべきであろう．"Horatian Ode" もまた有名．

16 **"*A winged sentry*"** 後に引用されている Vaughan の詩 "Peace" l. 3. 歩哨に立っている天使.

18 **Herbert,** George (1593-1633) 英国教会の牧師. "The Temple" という一巻の詩集に殆ど彼の全作品が収められている. 宗教詩にすぐれて居り, 「形而上詩人」に属する. "Virtue" はその傑作の一つであるが, "The Pully" "The Collar" 等も傑れた作品である.

19 **Crashaw,** Richard (1612?-49) 有名な反カトリックの説教者の子として生れ, 後にカトリックに改宗して司祭となった詩人. 宗教詩を集めた "Steps to the Temple" 一巻が主なる著作で, 大陸の神秘思想家の影響をうけ, 熱烈な信仰を吐露した抒情詩で有名である. "Hymn of the Nativity", "Saint Mary Magdalene", "Hymn to Saint Terresa" 等が名高い. 後の三篇は共に saints に訴えたものであるが, 二人とも女の聖人ではある.

104. 4 **angry**=Having the colour of an angry face, red (*O.E.D.* citing this line). **brave**=showy, fine (*O.E.D.*)

9 **A box where sweets ...** この一行は百花咲き乱れたうららかな春の日のうちつづく様を, 箱の中にきれいに並べてつめられた色とりどりのお菓子にたとえたもので, いわゆる「形而上的綺想」(metaphysical conceit) の一例である.

13 **gives**=of timber, to shrink from dryness. (*O.E.D.* citing this line)

105. 21 **range**=the act of ranging or moving about. (*O.E.D.*)

106. 4-5 **"God moves in a mysterious way"** Cowper については p. 3, l. 4 の註参照. この詩は "Olney Hymns" の第35番.

5 **Watts,** Isaac (1674-1748) "The Devine Songs for Children" 一巻によって記憶されている詩人. "Our God, our help in ages past" もその中の一篇である.

107. 8 **Lord Hervey,** John (1696-1743) 時の宮廷人で羽振りをきかせていた人. Pope と論争し, "Dunciad" と "Bathos" の中で Pope に "Lord Fanny" の名で, また "Epistle to Dr. Arbuthnot" の中では "Sporus" (Nero 皇帝の寵臣の名より) の名で叩かれている. 引用の詩行は後者の ll. 309-330 (中 313, 4 の二行省略). Pope が最も得意とした詩形はここに引用された heroic couplet と呼ばれるもので, iambic pentameter が二行宛韻をふんだものである.

18 **at the ear of Eve** Hervey が時の女王 Caroline の側近者であることを諷したもの.

familiar toad *cf.* "Paradise Lost," VI. 799-800. "Him (i.e.

Satan) there they (i.e. angels) found Squat like a toad, close at the ear of Eve."

23 **"Timon"** "Moral Epistles" IV. 趣味も分別もなくただ礼びらばかりをきる金持の典型. Duke of Chandos がモデルだという.

26 **Dryden,** John (1631-1700) 詩人. 劇作家. 批評家. 桂冠詩人となる. 劇としては悲劇の "All for Love" (『総べてを恋に』), 喜劇の "Marriage-à-la-Mode" (『当世風結婚』). 詩としては諷刺詩に "Absalom and Achitophel", 抒情詩に "Alexander's Feast" 等の傑作があり, 批評家としてはジョンソン博士から「英国批評の父」の称号をうけ, 一世を風靡した文豪であった. 英国古典派の源流をなす.

108. 4-5 **"The proper study of mankind is man"** Pope: "Essay on Man" 中の有名な一行. (Epistle II. 2)

14 **Swift,** Jonathan (1667-1745) 英国系アイルランド人. "Gulliver's Travels" で有名な人間嫌いの皮肉屋. 政界に雄飛せんとして失敗, 僧職に転じ相当の勢力を得たが保護者の Queen Anne の歿後は出世の望みも絶え, アイルランドに引退して土地の為につくした. 晩年は不遇の中に廃人となって死んだ. 古典と近代文学の優劣論を扱った諷刺的散文 "The Battle of the Books", カトリック教会, 英国教会, カルヴィン派 (即ち Puritans) の三教会の争いを諷した散文 "A Tale of a Tub" (勿論英国教会が一番ましで, カトリック教会が攻撃の矢面に立つ. カルヴィン派もやっつけられている), 二十年にわたる長い間彼が愛した女性 "Stella" への書簡集 "Journal to Stella" 等が有名である.

109. 6 **Milton** の "On the Late Massacre in Piedmont" Wordsworth の "On the Extinction of the Venetian Republic" のごとき sonnet がその代表的なものであろう.

10-11 **"The Wearing of the Green"** 緑色はアイルランドの別名 Green Erin から暗示されて生じたアイルランドを象徴する色. 英国に圧迫されたアイルランド人の不満と反抗を歌った歌である.

20-1 **One seventeenth-century poet** Dryden の "Upon the Death of Lord Hastings" をさすものらしいが, この詩では smallpox は真珠ではなく "gem" にたとえられている.

110. 13-4 **Two great poets, one Greek and one Latin** 前者は Hesiodos 後者は Virgil で, 各々 "Erga kai Hemerai" (『日と労働』), "The Georgics" (『農業詩』) を書いている. 因に後者は著者 Lewis の英訳がある.

20 **an English poet of the eighteenth century** John Philips

(1676-1709) という小詩人. "Cyder" (1708) は Virgil の「農業詩」に倣ったもの.

111. 16 **Shenandoah** [ʃénəndo(u)ə] Virginia と West Virginia を流れる河. この歌は Eugene O'Neill の劇, "Mourning Becomes Electra" の中で歌われている.

VIII

POEMS OF YESTERDAY AND TODAY

115. 11 **Robert Frost** (1875-1963) 現代米国第一流の詩人. New England に住み, 土地の風物を日常の用語で写実的に描いた詩が多い.

117. 24 **Joseph and Pharaoh's** [féərouz] **dream** Genesis XXXXI. (旧約聖書. 創世紀. 四十一章) に語られている有名な物語.

118. 21 "**dark Satanic mills**" ("Milton" f. 9, l. 6) mill とは工場を意味する.

25 **Kipling,** Rudyard [rʌ́djəd] (1865-1936) インド生れの英国の小説家. 詩人. インドを舞台とした小説. わが国でもおなじみの *Jungle Book, Kim* 等の小説, *Barrack-Room Ballads and other Verses* の如き詩集により, 大いに帝国主義を鼓吹した. 政治思想を別にすれば, 彼は男性的な愛すべき詩人である.

122. 4 **Housman,** A. E. (1859-1936) 古典学者. 詩人. Cambridge 大学のラテン文学教授であった. 詩としてはストア風な諦めと勇気を教えた "A Shropshire Lad" 一巻が代表作.

Bridges, Robert (1844-1930) 元桂冠詩人. Milton の詩形の研究家であり, そこから得た独自の詩形 (Neo-Miltonic Syllabics) を用いて傑作 "Testament of Beauty" (「美の遺言」) を書いた. 彼の手になる, 前出の G. M. Hopkins の遺稿の出版は, 詩壇に大きな反響をよびおこした.

de la Mare [deləmɛ́ə], Walter (1873-1956) 夢幻的な詩や小説で有名な作家. "The Listeners" という詩が最も有名であり, 彼の特色をよく現わしている. 小説には *Memoirs of a Midget, The Scarecrow and Other Stories* 等がある.

5 **Edward Thomas** (1878-1917) 1910年代の詩人達すなわち Georgian poets の詩風を守っていた代表的な詩人. はじめは旅行記や随筆を書いていたが, 前出 Frost と交わるに及んで詩を作り出した. 第一次大戦で戦死. *Poems* 一巻がある.

NOTES 165

IX

WHEN IS A POEM NOT A POEM?

123. 10 **"Abide with me"** Henry F. Lyte (1793–1847) の hymn.
124. 16 **wake** *cf.* p. 127, l. 9.
125. 7 **mon**=man.
  18 **"Man proposes..."** *cf.* "Man proposes, God disposes" (格言) この詩の作者は未詳.
129. 20-1 **"*streaming* London's *central* roar"** *cf.* p. 110, l. 8.
  24-5 **D. H. Lawrence** (1885–1930) 我国では "Lady Chatterley's Lover" を書いた小説家としてしか一般に知られていないが, 大多数の英国の小説家同様, 彼にも数冊の詩集がある. 文学者の本質は詩人にあるというのが英国でも, ドイツでも常識となっている. Lawrence は動物や植物の詩が好きであったらしい. この詩は "Bat" という題であるが, "Snake" という詩も有名である.

X

HOW TO ENJOY IT

138. 13 **...into your book** If you are interested to see the kind of poetry which famous men and women wrote when they were very young, you will find a great number of examples in Chapters 34 and 35 of *Early One Morning*, by Walter de la Mare. (原註)

検印省略

〈英文〉詩をよむ若い人に　　　〈版権取得〉

1954年3月10日　　1刷	定価(本体1800円＋税)
1969年4月20日　改訂1刷	
2008年2月29日　改訂76刷	

注釈者　　深瀬　基　寛
　　　　　川田　周　雄

発行者　　南　雲　一　範

発行所　株式会社　南雲堂
東京都新宿区山吹町361番地／〒162-0801
電話03　(3268) 2311（学校関係・営業部）
　　　　(3268) 2384（書店関係・営業部）
振替・00160-0-46863　ファクシミリ・03(3260)5425

013300　C-L10　　　　　　　　Printed in Japan

10日間完成英検準1級　一次試験対策 (解答付)　CD付
ECC編　A5 (176)　本体1600円
　最新出題傾向に合わせ、オリジナル問題を収録した問題集。短期間で自分の弱点を発見し、補強できるよう構成。最終章は模擬試験形式なので試験前の仕上げ学習に最適。

7日間完成英検準1級　二次試験対策 (解答付)　CD付
ECC編　A5 (128)　本体1500円
　面接問題にターゲットを絞った教材。面接で多く用いられる題材を取り上げ、丁寧な解説をつけた。付属のCDでリスニング力を上げつつ、本番さながらの試験を体験できる。

英検準1級対策模擬テスト　1次・2次試験 (解答付)　CD付
神田 弘慶　A5 (140)　本体1400円
　4回分のテストと詳しい解説をつける。
　筆記テストの傾向と対策・リスニングテストの傾向と対策・面接テストの傾向と対策。

英検準1級サクセスロード (解答付)　　別売CD1 (本体1614円)
尾崎 哲夫　A5 (154)　本体1243円
　「黒板」や「メモ」を使い、授業のような語り口調で丁寧に説明。文法項目ごとの章立てで、苦手な項目を何度もチェックでき、ムリムダのない効果的な学習ができる。

英検準1級エクスプレス (解答付)
尾崎 哲夫　四六 (170)　本体952円
　短期間に総仕上げができるように、出題されやすい問題をパターン別に列記した問題集。巻末の頻出ポイントは試験の直前に必読。自分の実力を試したい方におすすめ。

10日間完成英検2級　一次試験対策 (解答付)　CD付
ECC編　A5 (182)　本体1600円
　最新出題傾向に合わせ、オリジナル問題を収録した問題集。短期間で自分の弱点を発見し、補強できるよう構成。最終章は模擬試験形式なので試験前の仕上げ学習に最適。

7日間完成英検2級　二次試験対策 (解答付)　CD付
ECC編　A5 (128)　本体1500円
　面接問題にターゲットを絞った教材。面接で多く用いられる題材を取り上げ、丁寧な解説をつけた。付属のCDでリスニング力を上げつつ、本番さながらの試験を体験できる。

英検2級対策模擬テスト　1次・2次試験 (解答付)　CD付
神田 弘慶　A5 (140)　本体1400円
　4回分のテストと詳しい解説をつける。筆記テストの傾向と対策・リスニングテストの傾向と対策・面接テストの傾向と対策。

英検2級合格マニュアル [改訂版] (解答書着脱可)
市村 憲太郎 A5 (222) 本体1165円

合格の秘訣を短期間で取得できるよう、工夫された攻略本。英検の「急所」をポイント解説。問題演習で確実に力をつけることができる。英検のリーディング対策には最適の書。

英検2級サクセスロード (解答付)　　　別売CD1 (本体1650円)
尾崎 哲夫 A5 (158) 本体1146円

「黒板」や「メモ」を使い、授業のような語り口調で丁寧に説明。文法項目ごとの章立てで、苦手な項目を何度もチェックでき、ムリムダのない効果的な学習ができる。

英検2級エクスプレス (解答付)
尾崎 哲夫 四六 (216) 本体951円

短期間に総仕上げができるように、出題されやすい問題をパターン別に列記した問題集。巻末の頻出ポイントは試験の直前に必読。自分の実力を試したい方におすすめ。

10日間完成英検準2級　一次試験対策 (解答付) CD付
ECC編 A5 (192) 本体1600円

最新出題傾向に合わせ、オリジナル問題を収録した問題集。短期間で自分の弱点を発見し、補強できるよう構成。最終章は模擬試験形式なので試験前の仕上げ学習に最適。

7日間完成英検準2級　二次試験対策 (解答付) CD付
ECC編 A5 (112) 本体1500円

面接問題にターゲットを絞った教材。面接で多く用いられる題材を取り上げ、丁寧な解説をつけた。付属のCDでリスニング力を上げつつ、本番さながらの試験を体験できる。

英検準2級対策模擬テスト 1次・2次試験 (解答付) CD付
神田 弘慶 A5 (140) 本体1400円

4回分のテストと詳しい解説をつける。筆記テストの傾向と対策・リスニングテストの傾向と対策・面接テストの傾向と対策。

英検準2級合格マニュアル (解答書着脱可)
市村 憲太郎 A5 (204) 本体971円

合格の秘訣を短期間で取得できるよう、工夫された攻略本。英検の「急所」をポイント解説。問題演習で確実に力をつけることができる。英検のリーディング対策には最適の書。

英検準2級サクセスロード (解答付)　　　別売CD1 (本体1650円)
尾崎 哲夫 A5 (142) 本体1049円

「黒板」や「メモ」を使い、授業のような語り口調で丁寧に説明。文法項目ごとの章立てで、苦手な項目を何度もチェックでき、ムリムダのない効果的な学習ができる。

英検準2級エクスプレス (解答付)
尾崎 哲夫　四六 (160)　本体951円
　短期間に総仕上げができるように、出題されやすい問題をパターン別に列記した問題集。巻末の頻出ポイントは試験の直前に必読。自分の実力を試したい方におすすめ。

10日間完成英検3級　一次試験対策 (解答付)　　CD付
ＥＣＣ編　A5 (172)　本体1600円
　最新出題傾向に合わせ、オリジナル問題を収録した問題集。短期間で自分の弱点を発見し、補強できるよう構成。最終章は模擬試験形式なので試験前の仕上げ学習に最適。

7日間完成英検3級　二次試験対策 (解答付)　　CD付
ＥＣＣ編　A5 (86)　本体1500円
　面接問題にターゲットを絞った教材。面接で多く用いられる題材を取り上げ、丁寧な解説をつけた。付属のＣＤでリスニング力を上げつつ、本番さながらの試験を体験できる。

英検3級合格マニュアル (解答書着脱可)
市村 憲太郎　A5 (178)　本体971円
　合格の秘訣を短期間で取得できるよう、工夫された攻略本。英検の「急所」をポイント解説。問題演習で確実に力をつけることができる。英検のリーディング対策には最適の書。

英検3級サクセスロード (解答付)　　別売ＣＤ１ (本体1553円)
尾崎 哲夫　A5 (126)　本体951円
　「黒板」や「メモ」を使い、授業のような語り口調で丁寧に説明。文法項目ごとの章立てで、苦手な項目を何度もチェックでき、ムリムダのない効果的な学習ができる。

英検3級エクスプレス (解答付)　　別売ＣＤ１ (本体1845円)
尾崎 哲夫　四六 (154)　本体951円
　短期間に総仕上げができるように、文法項目ごとにわかりやすく簡潔に説明。ユニークでユーモア溢れる解説で、楽しく学習できるよう工夫されている。

TOEIC 600点突破！　パーフェクト英単熟語
小池 直己　四六 (250)　本体1165円
　過去に出題された問題の中から、特に実力アップのカギを握っている標準レベルの英単熟語を厳選。短期間で習得できるよう、語源等を示し、学習の効率化を図った。

TOEIC 730点突破！　パーフェクト英単熟語
小池 直己　四六 (246)　本体1165円
　過去に出題された問題の中から、特に実力アップのカギを握っている標準レベルの英単熟語を厳選。短期間で習得できるよう、語源等を示し、学習の効率化を図った。